KT-446-994

Anees Jung was born in Hyderabad. Her father, Nawab Hosh Yar Jung, was one of the principal advisers to the last reigning Nizam of Hyderabad, as well as a scholar, poet and crusader. As a child, she was brought up in seclusion but later went on to study at Osmania University and the University of Michigan, Ann Arbor, where she took a Master's degree in sociology and American studies.

Returning to India in the seventies, she began a career in journalism with *Youth Times*, a magazine she edited for the Bennet Coleman Group for seven years. She is now a columnist for several journals in India and abroad.

An inveterate traveller, she uses places—towns and villages, as the background for her meetings with the people of whom she writes. Among her books are *When a Place Becomes a Person, Unveiling India—A Woman's Journey, Song of India* and *Delhi, Agra, Jaipur*, a travel book she wrote with Khushwant Singh and Maharani Gayatri Devi of Jaipur.

Anees Jung lives in New Delhi.

This book is to be returned on or before the last date stamped below

Penguin Books India (P) Ltd., 210 Chiranjiv Towers, 43 Nehru Place, New Delhi-110019, India
Penguin Books Ltd., 27 Wrights Lane, London W8 5TZ, UK
Penguin Books USA Inc., 375 Hudson Street, New York, N.Y. 10014, USA
Penguin Books Australia Ltd., Ringwood, Victoria, Australia
Penguin Books Canada Ltd., 10 Alcorn Avenue, Suite 300, Toronto, Ontario M4V 3B2, Canada.
Penguin Books (NZ) Ltd., 182-190 Wairau Road, Auckland 10, New Zealand.

First published by Penguin Books India (P) Ltd. 1993

Typeset in Times Roman by FOLIO, G-68, Connaught Circus, New Delhi-110 001

To
my mother
who gave us the freedom
she never had

The sun is not allowed
To overtake the moon,
Nor does the night outpace the day.
Each in its own orbit runs.

—Sura Ya' Sin
The Koran
(Translated by N. J. Dawood)

Contents

Acknowledgements
Foreword   ix
The Doors of Hyderabad   *1*
Night of the New Moon   *5*
My Mothers Were Such Women   *9*
The Begum   *15*
The Begum's Niece   *22*
Parizad   *24*
Mahbubunissa   *28*
Sugra   *30*
Ameena   *33*
Rashida   *38*
Royal Mothers, Royal Daughters   *41*
Najma   *47*
Tayeba Begum   *50*
Gulbaden's Daughter   *53*
Mehdi Begum   *56*
Jilani Bano   *60*
Chand Babu's Daughters   *63*
The Nawab's Great Grand-Daughters   *65*
Bushra   *69*
Saleha   *73*
Nayab Jehan and Shah Jehan   *77*
Popli in the Desert   *81*
Shumsunissa   *87*
Mumtaz   *89*
Manubehn   *93*
Fatima Rehman   *96*
Akbari   *101*
Daughter of the Chenars   *104*
Wajida   *109*
Bano Begum   *112*
Kum Kum   *115*
Fatima   *118*
Beginnings in a Graveyard   *121*
Afterword   *124*

Acknowledgements

I offer my thanks to all the women quoted here whose words spoken often only suggested have helped me to evoke a sense of their lives.

Foreword

'You do not look like a Muslim woman,' says a European friend.

'Perhaps,' I tell him. 'I have not lived the life of an average Muslim woman.'

Having said that I begin to wonder. Is there a look to a Muslim woman? And is there a life she lives that is distinct from other women?

The traffic light turns green. A crowd surges across the street. In it I spot a face that I instantly recognize. It is that of a Muslim woman. How do I know? From the way it rests. There is a reticence in the eyes, a tentativeness in the step as if it is being measured not by anyone else but by herself. A veiled dignity surrounds her person. And yet she is an ordinary woman. I can tell she is poor from the burqa that she wears. Of faded black satin, it is frayed at the edges. She probably lives in a chawl in a back lane in Mahim I tell myself as she disappears into the street that houses the shrine of a Sufi saint.

Back home I meet the same face. When Kulsoom Bi opens the door I recognize the look—gentle, withdrawn, guarded. She has worked in my mother's house and I have watched her for long hours cooking, cleaning, going to the bazar, her head always draped. She even goes to sleep with her head draped. In the years I have known her I have never seen her hair. Nor have I known what she is all about. The bits that I know of her life, her early marriage, her unemployed husband, her insane daughter and her jhuggi that gets washed away every other monsoon—do not explain her look, her immense silence, one which I have taken for granted. For it is also the silence of my mother.

Deep wrinkles rest around my mother's large eyes. She carefully combs her silver-grey hair, covers herself with a white shawl and walks slowly with me down to the beach. I see her, a small shrunken figure against a vast grey ocean. 'It is so beautiful. I wish I could come here every day,' she says as if she has seen it for the first time. And yet I know she has heard its hissing sounds through long monsoon nights, watched it rise and recede through the years. But the ocean remains for my mother a view from a tiny window. As does much of a long life that she has accepted as a gift, one that she has never questioned but merely lived. The serenity that stems from such an acceptance is an aspect of her being, one that she shares with Kulsoom Bi and, perhaps, her nine-year-old daughter. What will you pray for, I had once asked the little girl while she was on her way to the shrine, buried behind the mêlée of a bazar in Bombay, of the Sufi saint Maqdoom Shah Baba.

'I will ask him to give me a burqa of black satin,' she had replied. She saw it as a gift and not a garb that would shut her bright eyes to the world. She would soon have to wear it like all girls in the neighbourhood. It was as much of a necessity as her clothes, one that girls inherited on marriage as part of their dowry to help them keep their honour intact.

It was purdah, I realized, that granted that look of withdrawal to the Muslim woman which I had perceived even in a crowd. Purdah, says a sociologist 'is one phenomenon which permeates women's lives to an extent that everything must be explained in the light of it.' Literally meaning curtain, purdah's ideological basis lies in certain verses of the Koran concerning modesty. Through the centuries, the rather mild injunctions to both sexes to be modest in dress and behaviour have evolved into a strict system of segregation, restricting women's activities and movements, pushing them into spaces where living acquires the tone of martyrdom, where to be mothers, wives and daughters becomes sanctified, where being Muslim provides the halo.

'I am a modern woman. But that does not mean I should be immodest. I can fight a battle wearing a burqa,' says one Muslim college student. And yet I see less of Islam in her daily rhythms, in her relations with her family and community. It still exists though on paper, in postulates to which she returns in times of crisis like going to a law court. Her Islam is no longer a force by which she lives each day. The extraneous demands of modern life push her to seek solutions that go beyond the framework of her faith.

In Delhi, I encounter a group of women who are gathered to protest against the Muslim Women's Bill that seeks to deprive Muslim divorcees of the right to claim maintenance beyond the iddat period of three months.

Unlike their veiled sisters, these women have come together to express a shared state of mind, one that each of them has individually achieved without veering away from the essence of their faith. They have dropped the veil but not the privacy it implies. Without irreverence, they have begun to question the paradox of their identity created by the pull between the Word of God and the words of men. Not since the time of the Prophet has the base of shared convictions been questioned as it is being done in the Muslim world today. Women are increasingly reassessing the reality they live in by redefining their status from the theological to the political. They have begun to reappraise traditional space, renegotiate old sanctions and articulate a reality that had for generations remained unarticulated. The questioning has changed the look in their eyes. It is perhaps that look which I have acquired which made my friend comment that I do not look Muslim.

I decided to look beyond this face that marks a Muslim woman. I began with my mother. In my own home, my own town. Then I travelled to towns where other Muslim women live. I went to Lucknow, heartland of Indian Islam, to Bhopal where the faith survives with dignity, nursing the memory of queens who ruled the state. I travelled distances—to the edges of the Rann of Kutch, into the desert where women practise a pristine Islam; down to the coastal region of Kerala where through the centuries different faiths have arrived by ocean routes. I found the Islam of Kerala as gentle as the green landscapes of the place. It seemed less insular, less vociferous. Its spirit was strong but its face gentle, mellower with the mingling. As it was in Bengal where women of Islam lived, receptive to streams of reform movements, and a vibrant Bengali culture.

I met women on several levels—in the city, living in ghettos, in hovels and in mansions and in the countryside where faith grows out of rivers and fields. I talked with women of letters who have analysed Islam, and watched those who live Islam without having read the Koran or the Hadith, the sayings of the Prophet. I met some who were rich and privileged and many who were poor and deprived among whom I found a faith at once intimate and fervent. Whatever the level and whichever the region, I discovered that the Muslim woman was not an insubstantial figure, disappearing behind a veil, but a person, more substantial than the look. She was a state of mind. The pages that follow are an attempt to reveal the feminine face of Islam as I have seen it in India.

June 1993   *Anees Jung*
New Delhi

NIGHT OF THE NEW MOON

The Doors of Hyderabad

'We closed the doors.' 'We stood against our doors.' 'We stay within doors,' is the cry of women everywhere. It seems like a story of doors. Lines of doors, fragile, wooden, some painted green, some fluorescent blue, some hung with curtains of sack, some bearing strings of tulsi leaves. Almost all bear locks. All that makes the doors are wooden planks with fragile chains that can neither resist a bang nor a barrage of stones. I knock on those that bear no locks, where women continue to live trapped in fear. Many of them have lost their men—a father, a husband, a son. 'Come and see our homes,' they say as I go into a row of identical hutments. I look into rock-bottom poverty, hordes of children, families huddled in spaces with no light, little air, but a consistent thread of hope. Fear has not robbed the women of courtesy nor a sense of grace that is part of the pervasive Hyderabad culture. The women offer tea and sweets, the children stare and smile. Traditionally cloistered, how do these women face tragedies imposed on them by an outside world that they have neither seen nor understood?

In one small white house an old man was beaten with chappals by a crowd. He died. His wife who was in the backyard, lives. She stares at his grey shirt that hangs on a nail in the wall with a packet of beedis sticking out of a pocket. 'I keep thinking that he has stepped out for his prayers and will return,' she mumbles, her eyes dry and vacant. In the wreckage on the floor lie tattered photographs of her grandchildren, bangles, pieces of a bright green sari and a picture of the Kabah, the cube-like building at the centre of the mosque at Mecca, torn out of its frame. 'I feel suffocated,' says her neighbour, an elderly woman. 'I have not been outside these walls for weeks. Even when I step out in my backyard, I am afraid. They looted the fruits from the trees. I sit and chant my beads. Taking Allah's name keeps away the fear.' Somewhere beyond the wall is her lost husband who has not returned home since the riots broke out in the mandi.

'I can't sleep,' says Zahida, a young woman who lost a son. Her large eyes are red and swollen for she cannot stop crying. 'I keep waking up to listen to the azaan and for the morning to dawn. I keep praying that he comes in my dreams and I try to sleep. It has been months and I have not seen him even in my dreams. I watch the street hoping he will walk down.' She is referring to her eighteen-year-old son who was shot in police firing. He was her first-born, a son who was also a brother, a friend, a very special person. 'He always wore freshly laundered clothes and his shoes were always polished,' she wails, wiping her tears with her ragged veil. 'He could touch a sheep and know its weight. He was a good butcher, also a good poet. He would sit for hours on the terrace and write his ghazals. He won prizes in poetry competitions.' She shows the prizes, the pictures of him standing on stage, reciting poems. 'I helped him into his shirt as he was leaving. Why did I not grab him from the back and stop him? If only I had known that he would not return. I am not even so big that God should put me to such a test. I am an ordinary woman.'

Are you not angry? I ask another lady whose lawyer son was stabbed to death as he emerged from a mosque after his afternoon prayers. 'Angry with whom?' she questions, her voice devoid of rancour. With God? 'He is the only God I have. If I get angry with Him to whom will I turn? God is not a Chief Minister who can be dismissed and replaced.' Such abiding faith in the face of her gravest tragedy is baffling. I soon see however, this sort of faith is intrinsic to the culture of most Muslim women. 'If my beloved son is taken away it must be part of God's design, one that only He knows, which goes beyond human understanding. If He inflicts a tragedy on you then He also gives you the strength to bear it. He knows what strength each human being has. We are just mortals.'

Surrender to the will of Allah is the basis of her faith. In it is wrapped her quiet strength, her will to live on. A curtain of serenity hangs over her home. It does not feel like a house where a son had been killed a month ago. The sound of a child's tricycle breaks the quiet. A portrait of an ancestor in formal headgear hangs above the entrance door in the manner of an announcement, informing one of the age of the house and its tradition. Those who live in it know and understand the ebb and flow of changes. 'Which of us will live forever?' asks the bereaved mother. 'We are all travellers in this journey of life and we get down at different stations.'

These are the first of many such scenes that I am to encounter. The story is the same—of sorrow and tears, of loss and a deep pain. Solace lies in prayer, and fortitude is born of a strong faith that has no room for anger or recrimination. These women are stoics. They seek no exits out of a shuttered world. Sharing the same time and planet are women who talk of choices and fight to create them. Writes Liv Ullman: 'I am learning that if I just go on accepting the framework of life that others have given me, if I fail to make my own choices, the reason for my life will be missing. I will be unable to recognize that which I have the power to change.'

Words of courage that ring distantly. Is it possible to find one's reason for life when its framework has already been worked out? How can a woman born confined recognize what should be changed? Isn't the power to change itself an energy that first needs to be located, then nurtured and expressed? For many of the Muslim women I meet the reason for their lives was worked out fourteen hundred years ago, in a Bedouin Islam. It remains not only a faith sealed in the covers of a book but is a living, shared tradition. It is not part of a structure but is the structure within which they live savouring age-old certainties. From among them I see two stereotypes emerge: There is the gracious lady in the old mansion who has read, imbibed and is living in the finest traditions of Islam, and the numberless illiterate women living in the confines of poverty and degradation who have not read the Book but feel the urgent need to cling to it. Their lives are not sad, pretty stories of another time. They are our time. As men raise the battle cry of Allah and tear a world apart, its centre remains still like the mourning eye of a storm. It is where the women live, to whom God is love, mercy and compassion. In the grime of their lives I see patches of light, of hope and affirmation; a poetry that the Hindus trace to a devotion called shradha, which the Muslims call imaan, a faith that surrenders to the will of one God.

Night of the New Moon

'Nana's Islam was simple and fragrant'

As a child I climbed the highest terrace of our house to sight the new moon. Would it rise or would its crescent curve evade our eyes? It was a night of waiting, of not knowing, of wondering. When it wanly appeared it was hailed as a great sign from heaven. From the glittering minarets of mosques the grave mullahs would announce that the moon had been sighted. The old cannons in my childhood city would boom. The new moon signalled a beginning, a transition. With it Ramzan arrived changing the patterns of our days and nights, of eating and drinking, of loving and living. Ramzan is the month of God, said mother. He revealed His Word to the Prophet in this month and that was the glorious Koran. The gates of heaven remain open during the holy month, believed my mother.

'Your prayers are heard, your wishes fulfilled, your sins forgiven. It is the month to be good and charitable to the poor, think pure thoughts and not tell a single lie.' I do not remember if I did not tell a lie or if I was really good. I never knew the fullness of Ramzan for I neither fasted nor prayed. I did participate in the culture of the month though, delighting in awaking for sehri, the meal eaten before sunrise that signals the beginning of the fast. '*Sehri karo utho Ramzan ke rozedaro*,'—Come for sehri, all you who fast for Ramzan—called the man who belonged to the night, his voice ringing strong and clear like a bell in the still night. We never saw his face, just heard his voice. We imagined him as an old man with soft sad eyes and a flowing white beard, the kind that fakirs have. The one who woke to his call every morning was Nana, an old grand-aunt who lived in the house with us.

Across the span of years she remains before my mind's eye as a very gentle woman, who lived invisibly, whose silence was itself an ibadat, a prayer. She was a widow, was always dressed in a thick white sari that she washed herself daily, spreading it out on the terrace, the only outdoors she knew. She fasted all the thirty days of Ramzan. She would keep a bowl of rice and vegetables, covered with a plate, beside her bed. She did not want to disturb the household when she awoke for sehri.

Before the white thread of dawn appeared she would eat the cold rice, seated on her bed in the dark. During the day she touched no food and water, listened to no music. It was a denial of all her five senses. When the black thread of night appeared she broke her fast with a date or a pinch of salt and water. Iftaar, the breaking of the fast after sunset, was as simple a ritual for Nana as was sehri. She expected no feast nor did she want anyone to treat her in a special way throughout the day. Fasting was not a burden for her nor did she impose it on others. While she fasted she moved around the house doing what she did on ordinary days. The denial and restraint that the month of fasting is supposed to stir in a person were qualities natural to her. She had lived an entire life in a manner that people try to live during the thirty days of Ramzan. All months, for Nana, were ordained by God. Through the day she prayed as if she was truly in the presence of God. We watched her bowed over a fat book for hours. She chanted from the Koran the way the Prophet must have, centuries ago, when the Book was revealed to him. Her sounds reverberated through the house chasing the other echoes. Her voice rose in a gentle crescendo and fell, hushing our chatter. Unaware of the meaning or majesty of the words she recited we listened. At night those sounds turned into stories that lulled us to sleep. During Ramzan she would prepare bowls of fruits and salty delicacies and send them to the neighbourhood mosque where poor rozedars congregated. 'Food should be shared with the poor who have no home to go, who come to the mosque as if to a home,' Nana would say. Many little mosques in the city turned into homes where iftaar was shared as readily as faith.

I denied myself that feeling for I did not fast the way Nana did. Years later I continue to be the watcher though a more involved one. My name, because it is Muslim, figures on the guest lists of iftaar parties held ceremonially in the capital. Like me, many who are invited are not rozedars. Their token presence is meant to reinforce the secular rituals. Nana's Islam was simple, fragrant and elegant. As was her face, her figure, her manner. In fasting and in celebration Nana remained the same. The new moon did not change the constancy of her days.

Today I sight the new moon in Delhi's smog-filled skies. High terraces open to the heavens are a thing of the past as is Nana for she is long dead. Eid no longer means a celebration that marks the long wait. On the calendar that hangs in my study the festival is not even marked. It is a Japanese calendar. I emerge for my morning walk as I do on any ordinary day. Sitting in his garden chair my neighbour says 'Eid Mubarak.' His voice lacks the festive note. Is it Eid, I ask him. 'Don't you know?' he quips. 'What kind of a Muslim are you?'

What kind indeed, I wonder as I proceed on my daily route, past the sweet shop that is closed, along a wide empty road into the wilderness of a park where hidden peacocks call to each other. It is not a mating call, but a cry of anguish. Like the muffled voice in my own heart. Why does a celebration for which I would wait thirty days no longer announce itself? Have I chosen not to wait for it or has it chosen to bypass me? Do festivals choose their points of celebration? Do they happen only in homes where families live and in localities where the faithful are visible? I live alone and am the only Muslim in the neighbourhood. To experience the fervour of celebration I get into a car and drive out to Jama Masjid, along roads where big and small men dressed in crisp new clothes are on their way to the Idgah where they will stand in rows and offer prayers. I cannot be part of their togetherness for I am a woman, forbidden to pray alongside others in a mosque.

To feel one with the spirit of celebration I walk in the bazar that circles the mosque. Women enclosed in burqas have emerged from their courtyards to buy perfume, fruits, flowers. And, of course, sivayan, the fine vermicelli used for preparing sheer-korma, traditionally served on the occasion of Eid. Are you from around here? asks the perfumer seeing me alone and unveiled. And in the next breath boasts that his shop dates back to the time of the Mughal Emperor Akbar. The references here have not changed nor has the spirit of the time. But it has with me. I no longer feel part of the ritual that binds a community. I make my own norms for a celebration. And that no longer happens on the night of the new moon.

Time has moved and I with it. To live in my time I have evolved my own faith. 'You do not question a gift,' my mother would say. 'You receive it with both your hands, gather it to your bosom, cherish it and live by it.' Now, the prayers that my mother taught me do not fully answer my questions. Nor do they subdue unnamed fears. I have rolled up my prayer rug and put it away. I will bring it out when I discover the connection between her prayers and my life.

My Mothers Were Such Women

'I never figured them out'

If I were to paint a portrait of my mother it would be in the colour green. Not the green of the vibrant paddy fields that circled her house and her growing years but the green of Islam—sombre, unchanging, inspiring awe, evoking mercy and compassion. As she looks back at her life, a picture emerges that did not paint itself but was painted. She has lived eighty long years patterned out by Him. Even the fact of her surviving a storm she owes to His mercy.

It was September, at the dawn of this century when Hyderabad was caught in the eye of a storm. It was a black night at the end of the days of the moon. The river Musi rose high enough to drown an elephant. Its waters billowed like an ocean, surged over roofs, swept away bridges, trees, men. They swirled away from the river bed and lapped on the doorsteps of the houses that lined its banks. One such house was that of my grandmother who was nursing a girl forty days old. To save her from the river's wrath, my grandmother went around the house with a piece of charcoal, writing the name of Allah on the walls so that they would not be washed away. The walls stood. As did the faith of a simple God-fearing woman. The girl who survived was the gift of a mother's imaan, a faith woven in total surrender to the will of Allah.

Like many women in Hyderabad my mother was not brought up to choose how she would live. As a young girl she lived cloistered in a farmhouse. Whilst my grandmother made her daily rounds of the paddy fields, the toddy trees and the mango groves, my mother stayed in her room growing older, reading religious books, novels, poetry.

Every year the paddy turned tall and green, the farmhouse hummed. Every summer the mangoes ripened in the groves. The farmers' wives sat through long afternoons and packed them in baskets for the city. One such summer my mother turned sixteen. In her room, in front of the large round mirror, she would stand and watch herself, the glow in her cheeks, the dream in her large beautiful eyes. Through the chilman, the fine cane curtain that veiled her from the outside but not the outside from her, she would often gaze at my father, a constant visitor to the farm. 'I just liked looking at him. I never really knew why.' She would quietly open a book that carried his photograph and greet it with a salaam every morning. Little did she know that one day he would be her husband.

Once married she had little time to sit and look at herself in the mirror. She forgot the dream in her eyes and lost the glow in her cheeks. By the time she was twenty she had had two children. And every year, for the next five years, another child. Her children became the focal point of her life. Her days were spent cooking their favourite foods, sewing their clothes, nursing their colds and coughs. In the long winter evenings she would tell them stories she had read in her room and learnt from her deeply religious father. The ecstasy and turbulence of their growing years—their small pleasures, their big and small moments, examinations, successes, marriages, their new homes and their children—one cycle slipped into another.

And so the years passed, each day seemingly the same but momentous in the circle of her family life. With the children scattered, and her world shrunk, she now sits on a bed holding in her shrivelled hands the strings of several remote lives. She can no longer write letters or read those that she receives. On the telephone the voices of her dear ones have begun to sound faint.

Eighty years have shrivelled her body but not her mind or her spirit. Her wrinkles do not rebel, they rest gently on her face, her hands, her arms. Her laugh has the ripple of youth, her almond-shaped eyes, now watery and without vision, continue to dream, for others.

My mother was a creature of a land which saw God in earth and sky, in the cycle of seasons and the wheel of life and death. A godless land to a Hindu is a dead land. Though she lived secluded behind the walls of a house within which Islam prevailed, the landscapes that surrounded her were washed by another fervour. They helped her to know the colour of fields in bloom and the strength of rains for which the village prayed. Hearing the song in the distance she knew it was festival time when a goddess decked better than a queen, was carried in procession. Much in the same manner the alams, the insignia of the Prophet's family, journeyed to the stream to be put in a watery grave on the tenth day of Muharram.

Rituals of another faith were equally respected in my mother's birthplace. Butchaiah, the village headman, a Hindu, raised a gate at the shrine of the local Sufi saint. He would distribute sherbet to the poor in memory of the saint on the day he took purdah (died). Saidulu, a Hindu mason, carried the prefix of a Muslim name in his memory. His mother had prayed to the saint for the birth of a son. When the baby was born she named him after the saint. Beliefs and festivals were shared in her village across communal lines. On the day of the new moon, the Ramzan Eid, my grandmother gave the gift of a sari and green bangles to the Hindu peasant women to signify an auspicious beginning. The Islam of my mother lived in a moral universe where ties of kinship reached out to all living men and women, to the rivers and fields and rocks.

Miles away in Bilgram, a small place in the plains of northern India where my father became a man, the spirit of the milieu was much the same. His roots did not lie in the land but in scholarship. His family was among the first inhabitants who settled in Bilgram during the time of King Altamish. The village drew its inspiration from a feudal era. It had its mansions and its cool springs, its fields of mangoes and melons. Every other home nursed a scholar or a poet. Craftsmen thrived in the village and when Madnayak sang the *Megh Raag*, memories of the legendary Tansen were revived.

My father, like other little boys in the village, learnt his alphabet from a maulvi called Sharafat Ali. In his free time he herded the maulvi's ducks. On the day of Eid he presented the revered teacher with a nazar, a gleaming silver coin. From Pandit Deep Narayan he learnt his arithmetic and spent long hours at gymnastics. But like a good Muslim boy he would not stand on his head for fear of pointing his feet to Heaven where Allah resided. At school he shared his bench with two Hindu boys, Misri Lal and Radhe Shyam. They taught him to wear a dhoti and escorted him to Bhole Chacha, the village barber, for his first shave. That was a time when caste and creed were not as important as the bonds that tied a people to the geography and culture of a place. No riot erupted then if a band played in front of a mosque nor was there a fight over the possession of a pipal tree under which sat a flaming orange Hanuman.

Bilgram was not to remain that way for long. By the time my father grew a moustache the village failed to recognize him and he the place of his birth. The mansions of the gentry began to crumble behind screens of fragrant smoke that rippled out of their hookahs. The poor became poorer. As young girls turned into women there was little money for their marriage or dowry. Sensitive to the decay some families left Bilgram. To be muhajirs, to migrate in search of a better life, was part of the old belief. My father's family migrated south to the courts of princes carrying with them their foods and flavours, their books and the name of Bilgram. Responsive to scholarship and enlightened thought, Hyderabad welcomed the Bilgramis.

My father came into his own, earned himself a title from the last reigning Nizam, built a mansion with a garden to raise a family and lived life with the aesthetics of a poet and a nobleman. He was not a Koran-toting Muslim though he had spent years studying it. Critical of the dogma and ritual that had entered Islam, he believed in humanism as the basis of his faith. But his life failed to escape the trappings of a feudal Muslim ethos. Like gentlemen of his time he did not hesitate to take a few wives in accordance with the Shariat, the Koranic law that guided the lives of men more than the women.

His first wife was a woman from the village, a few years older than himself. As a young man he had become an unwilling victim of his parents' decision. The story goes that on the wedding night when he lifted the veil to see the bride's face he exclaimed, 'She is old enough to be my mother.' Soon after he left her and his parental home. While he travelled into a larger world, she stayed in his parents' home, gave birth to a daughter who turned into a gawky woman without ever knowing her father. He remained for her a loved but mythical figure. Both carried his name and lived small, contented lives with the money he sent them.

My father travelled, his career soared and he took a second wife. She was Mohemmedi Begum, daughter of one of Hyderabad's gentry. She bore him no children. As their large home turned into an empty shell, my father amused himself with the children of relatives who visited the house. One of them was a young niece of his wife, a shy girl with large, limpid eyes who would often visit them in the city. He would tell her stories and bring her chocolates and Golden Puff Biscuits. She was ten then and he twenty-eight. In the years that followed, while he moved between the princely courts of Rampur and Bhopal, he did not see the girl. She was in her village growing older under the shade of banyans, watching the lush paddy fields and the splendour of summer mangoes. On a visit to her aunt—her 'Khalamma', a term for an aunt as dear as a mother—she again encountered my father. She was now a young woman, tall and sinuous, her eyes full of rainbows. He could no longer bring her chocolate or tell her stories. The desire to be with her, however, remained. Within a year he married her. Her aunt moved away to a small house in the old city. There was no communication between the small and the big houses, except fragmented tales that visitors carried.

A decade passed. My father's third wife bore him seven children. I am third in the series. When a son was born after a long wait my mother said, 'I must visit Khalamma and break the good news.' Said my father, 'You will be met with a dagger.' Instead she was met by the Book. The aunt, now her souten, a co-wife, stood on the porch holding the Holy Koran in her two hands. That's the way people came together if they had not met for more than twelve years. My mother walked under the Koran that her aunt held high. The two women then embraced and shed tears. 'Now I have a son,' said Mohemmedi Begum taking the baby boy in her arms. From that day on she became Ammi to all of us. When she died an old woman she was already a widow. As was my mother. Yet she performed Ammi's last rites the way my father would have if he had lived.

My mother continues to cherish her aunt's memory. The relationship between the two women never soured despite the fact that they shared a husband. Sabr was their way of life. The Koran explains sabr as a quality that implies acceptance, restraint, patience and grace. It is a quality that every Muslim woman imbibes as an essential tenet of her faith. My two mothers nurtured and savoured this quality, remained 'good' despite themselves. Like many women of their generation, they were not just born noble but were rigorously groomed to be so. In that time to be ambitious, even for one's personal happiness, was considered bad form. To negate one's greed and desire, to give up for others and sacrifice for a larger peace, to guard one's honour and that of the family, were precepts drilled into every Muslim girl. To be one of four wives was also a norm she was groomed to accept as a sanctified part of her role. It was a condition in which she was born and lived, which she had no reason to question or mystify. To probe it would have amounted to sacrilege. My mothers were such women. I never figured them out.

The Begum

'One cries before Allah not before other human beings'

Meeting a Begum miles away in a desert kingdom is to come face to face with the spirit of a traditional if crumbling Islam. Steep stone steps reminiscent of a fortress lead up to a large square room whose blue walls have begun to peel. The haveli is as desolate inside as outside. Even in its heyday, when its walls glinted with mirrors it was, in the words of the Begum, her 'golden cage.' She never stepped out of it. Nor does she today. Few call on her. She calls on no one. She lives invisibly as if guarding a secret.

On a small sofa, she sits as though posing for a photograph. She is dressed in shades of grey, a dupatta draping her head and much of her body. White chintz curtains flap lazily in the desert air, stirring her veil and revealing a head of henna-dyed hair. A turquoise pendant studded discreetly with rubies winks through the gauze-like chiffon taking one back to the age of gems and jewels when women were resplendent, lending zinat, the quality that decorates and blesses the house. Few of them remain.

Two girls, dressed in the manner of small-town urbanites, glide into the room carrying trays of tea, biscuits and bunches of yellow bananas. They are her nieces, children of a democratic era. Placing the trays on the varnished coffee table they withdraw. The eats are simple but the gesture formal. Yet none of that formality clings to the Begum. Hers is a natural dignity which is more an aspect of her nature than one imposed by a royal life style.

Sixty-seven, gently alert, she is the last of a generation of Begums who was an intimate witness to an era that knew power, riches and unsurpassed splendour. Her husband, like all princes in India, was stripped of his title, his privy purse and his privileges. As his state lapsed into oblivion he withdrew into the seclusion of his palace. The Begum remained untouched by the loss. She had her faith. 'It is Islam that gives us shaoor, the desire to know and live in the world. And that has guided me throughout life,' she says simply. Her voice is soft and intimate, her manner spontaneous. She is open about her inner life that was groomed by the ideals of Islam, discreet when she talks about her life in the palace. Fifty years of regality recede as she looks back at her childhood spent in a small town encompassed by pristine Islam. Memories of youth kindle a warmth and togetherness. Those linked with the palace are guarded. They sum up an experience that she never really absorbed, that remained outside of her.

'I was brought up in a middle-class, conservative family,' she begins in the manner of a story teller. 'My father and uncles were men of religion. My mother was illiterate but very wise. Her understanding of things stemmed from her faith and her experience. She taught me the namaz when I was four years old. Sitting in my father's lap I learnt to recite the verses of the Koran.' To have a male teacher in the house was taboo. The maulvi who was selected to teach the Begum the Koran was an old man who would doze off while teaching. The Begum was brought up in strict purdah and was mostly alone, not allowed even to befriend the children of her aunts and uncles lest they led her astray. 'Though father loved us girls we held him in fear. I was very close to my mother. It was she who taught me the values by which she lived—compassion, patience, restraint, adab-e-mehfil, adab-e-buzurgi, how to conduct oneself among people, with elders, with the poor and the less privileged.'

Spoken endearingly, memories of her mother evoke a form that is spare but strong. I see a figure pervading a home and a courtyard, a family, a clan. In her memories I trace outlines of my own mother and grandmother. And hers emerges as a fair Pathan woman wrapped in a chadar, filling spaces, walied by brick. 'Poor Pathan women would arrive at her doorstep hiding their poverty in the blackness of the night. Welcoming them she would disappear in the kitchen to pack small bags of rice, lentils, salt and chillies. 'You have left your bags by the door,' she would say, referring to the bags she had discreetly placed at the doorway.

The women would take the bags and go away to feed their waiting children. And when Pathan men came into the baithak, the men's drawing-room, she would make paans and send them out. In each paan she would fold a silver coin. 'Tell them to take it home and eat,' she would instruct the bearer. She wanted no one to know what she gave away. And she did not want those who received her charity to be embarrassed. 'That was her way of giving,' says the Begum. 'When you give with one hand, the other hand should not know, the Prophet has said. Watching her we naturally understood the dictum.'

From a simple God-fearing home the Begum found herself transported to the rich and leisured world of a Nawab's palace. She had not set eyes on her husband before marriage. The day he first entered her room she turned cold from head to foot, she tells me. For six months she dared not speak. 'It was not dislike, just fear. Even when I began to talk I was never alone with him. There were guards night and day and they were all women. No man was allowed in the palace. Even a pregnant woman was stopped at the gate lest she was carrying a male in her womb.'

Was such strict purdah justified? 'Yes,' she mumbles, leaving me baffled. Seclusion, I realize, is part of her conditioning, one that she does not question. She quotes a story to reinforce her belief. 'A man once saw the Caliph Umar rushing down the street with a cut on his head, bleeding. "What happened? You had gone visiting your daughter," the man asked. To which the Caliph replied that his daughter was alone in the house. "So what? Isn't she your daughter?" questioned the man. "She was alone," answered the Caliph. "The devil is with everyone. So I fled to protect myself and her".'

However good, woman has a tendency to go astray, repeats the Begum. So controls are necessary for her. And yet, the Begum concludes: 'No man can dare if a woman is not willing. In her rests the strength of bigadna and sawarna, to mar or make the world.'

The Begum never stepped out of the world of women. In

childhood it was her mother. After marriage it was other women, who were her husband's wives, some were Begums, some discarded wives who had lost the Nawab's favour. It took all kinds to make the harem. Many poor women were sent to the palace by the state's Shariat department. If they were pretty they became the Nawab's qawases or casual wives. A simple nikah ceremony made her his wife lending her protection and respectability. Many, however, remained in the wings waiting to draw the Nawab's attention. Often they languished and grew old without love or children. '*Doosrey ki nafs ko maarna gunah hai*,' broods the Begum, as if to herself. Though she admits that suppressing another's natural desires is a sin in her faith, she raises no questions. 'If a man has the physical strength and can treat them equally he has the right to take more than one wife,' she asserts, stressing in the next breath that according to the Koran even a blade of grass should be split equally so that each of the four wives gets an equal share. 'I was his favourite Begum but I insisted that he treat the others equally, and talk to each of us when we sat around him. "Will it not hurt you?" he would ask. No, I would assure him. God's command is more important than my hurt. And don't think it did not hurt. But I had trained myself to bear it.'

She remained alone but was never lonely. The palace buzzed with activity all the year round. There were festivals and celebrations, games of cards and chauser, evenings of song and verses, hunts, picnics in the summer by the riverside. The Begums would travel in curtained palanquins and luxuriate in tents screened with fragrant khus chilmans. Parties rang through the night. There was laughter, jokes, and veiled insults. Behind the colour, fragrance and merriment raged a subtle violence. The Begum, though a part of it, remained apart. 'Stay like a duck in water,' her mother would advise. 'When a duck flies away its wings remain dry.'

Many of the women, recalls the Begum, stooped to envy, malice and evil deeds. They dabbled in intrigue, back-biting, even black magic. The servants of one Begum would set the children against those of another. 'I could never bear a child,' confides the Begum. 'Each of my pregnancies was mysteriously aborted. I knew what was going on but I said nothing. Like a tongue in a set of thirty-two teeth I set a lock to my mouth. I never talked. My word could have been command but I never gave it. Nor did I complain to the Nawab. When I wanted to cry I would go into my room. One cries before Allah not in front of other human beings. Sometimes Nawab Saheb would see my red eyes and enquire. Just a slight fever I would tell him. "From where did you acquire such sabr?" he would often ask. If a majboor or a helpless person is slapped and he stays quiet that is not sabr. But if you slap an equal who is in a position to slap you back but does not, that restraint is sabr.

'Some of the other Begums too had this gift. One of them who was deeply religious raised a mosque at every place she visited. Another built a serai for travellers in Medina. I made neither friends nor enemies. Don't be so sweet that you can be swallowed nor so bitter than you can be spat out, my mother would say. I stayed separate from them but remained close to my imaan. That was my only protection.'

The Nawab who brought her to his palace as his fourth and final Begum rewarding her with a long title has long been dead. As is his brother who later became the Nawab and also her second husband. She gave them no heir. And yet she remained a favourite Begum revered for her qualities of dignity, detachment and silence.

What do fifty years of silence do to a woman? 'I feel old and forget much,' the Begum says in a voice that trails into a whisper. 'With the kind of suffering I have known I should have long perished. My prayers kept me alive. When Allah gives life no power in the world can take it away. All those who conspired against me are dead. I am alive and am still the Begum. Our destiny is made in the mother's womb. We arrive with a gift from God. I could neither groom nor enhance my life with the gifts God gave me. It was partly my weakness, partly imposed. One should not surrender to taqdeer, one's fate. There is also tabdeer, the wisdom to perceive and change.'

She quotes the story of the Prophet asking Umar where he had left his camel. Umar had answered 'In God's care.' To which the Prophet rejoined: 'First make all arrangements that are within your power. Tie up the camel. Then leave him in God's care.'

'That is tabdeer,' explains the Begum. 'Do your best and leave the rest to God. What He bestows on us we should accept and be happy. If He gives wealth we should bow in gratitude. If He chooses to keep us poor we should accept that too. God lives among the poor. Never let your heart be empty of God. Only He stays. All else is fanna, that extinction which marks the end of all human journeys.'

If God were to send you back into this world for another lease of life, would you accept the same life? I ask her. 'That's not our belief' she says in a tone of disapproval. A hypothetical question, I assure her. 'In that case, no,' she mutters. And the same man as husband? 'No,' she says raising her voice. For a brief moment the mask falls. She looks old and tired. The glint of the turquoise pendant fails to cheer her presence. 'But where can I go now?' she asks looking distantly out of a curtained window. 'I feel claustrophobic. I want my solitude. I want to be so poor that I become invisible. I can do nothing. Time has run out.'

I leave her sitting on the sofa as the metal clock on the blue wall ticks away. Outside the palace, dogs bark. The compound is desolate. Along the sun-stained street, by another gate, the entrance to a palace in ruins, stands a burly man dressed in a white muslin shirt. He is the present Nawab, I am told. The late Nawabs had no sons. The gaddi thus passed from one brother to another. The one who stands by the gate, like a commoner, inherited a sleeping title without the wealth and the gun salutes. Like many men in his state he spends time writing poetry and fishing in the river. Six thousand such royal men and women are loosely joined in the Amiri association that meets occasionally to settle family disputes, divorce cases and legal problems. Gone are the days when the family gathered for fun and games. The men have lost their ease despite the languor they exude, dressed in finely crafted muslin kurtas and the colourful batwas that they carry filled with paan masala. The women who have remained in the cloistered rooms kill their time gossiping and playing cards. The younger ones have begun to leave. A few, I learn, have ended up as mistresses of jewellers in bigger cities. 'Time stopped here a long time ago,' says one native. 'Those who wanted to live have chosen to go away.'

I travel back through brown, tired landscapes that once made up the Begum's kingdom. For she had a title, and commanded half as many gun salutes as the ruling Nawab. Yet no one in the kingdom set eyes on her. She remained for her subjects an illusion like the rasiya, an unknown beloved in whose honour a small monument was raised on top of the hill that guards the city gates.

The Begum's Niece

'I flew out of the golden cage'

 Less than a hundred kilometres away but further in spirit, lives a young woman who is the grand-niece of the Begum. She lives in a small rented house and works in a travel agency. Neither her looks nor her carriage suggest the Begum's nobility. Only her speech has echoes of the eloquence that one associates with the well-born. Dinner in her home is hospitable but simple. We eat in the sitting room, balancing the plates on our laps, while a television blares in the next room. The decor is sparse and uninteresting. A few old embroideries that hang prominently on walls sullenly forge her royal connections. She apologizes for not serving me in the dining room; she has none. Cruel time, she mourns, has vandalized her heritage: the Persian carpets, the stuffed tigers, the glass and porcelain have been sold off or auctioned. Something of that grandeur must have remained in your person, I suggest. Not treasures that deck a house but qualities of head and heart that remain an aspect of the Begum? She looks embarrassed and turns her attention to the platter of sizzling biryani.

'There was little of that even in her time,' she quips, her voice sharp. 'The Begum perhaps was an exception. I left the palace to go to boarding school and returned only when I was seventeen. Everything as a child seemed to me a fable—the palace was lovely, the women beautiful. They wore gorgeous clothes. Fine net kurtas and gauze-like dupattas sparkled with gems that beamed inside the net dresses like fireflies. They wore their pyjamas tight enough to reveal their curves. I was charmed by the way they lived—eating good food, wearing fine clothes for the pleasure of the Nawab and for each other—spouting jokes and poetry.

'On my return I saw the same women with other lenses. I was shocked when I heard them speak to each other in loud voices. Their jokes were lewd, often cruel. Many of them led licentious lives with a male tucked away for their secret pleasures. He was often a relative who was paid, and his family, if he had one, was supported. In this so-called purdah world nothing was taboo, no one was shocked, not even the children. But when I spoke of my life in the convent many of the women were surprised. They could not visualize a life outside the palace, could not distinguish the good from the bad. Those who were sensitive turned into themselves, waited for someone to arrive and take them out of the golden cage. After a year I began feeling like them and wanted to run away. The best way was to get married. But the question was to whom? A cousin used to visit. He was handsome and looked polished. In such a milieu he seemed God-sent. I decided to marry him and go away but my mother was against it. He lacked breeding, she warned. I did not hear her. A week after marriage I realized my mistake.'

Two sons were born to her in the years of her short, tumultuous marriage. He then abandoned her for another woman, who was once a maid in a royal household. She sought no divorce. She found a job and moved to the city. She saw him when he visited the city, went with him to parties for the sake of the family image, and for the sake of her children. She has accepted her destiny but without the serenity that marks the life of her grand-aunt. She moulds her life though with a strength that has roots not in a faith but in herself.

'I flew out of the golden cage,' she says with a nervous laugh. 'I have opened the door and got a glimpse of the outside. Now I stare at another door that may be slammed in my face.'

Parizad

'It is suffering that gave me strength'

Seven girls sit on a festooned stage, stooped under the weight of bridal finery. The glitter of their red veils is not of gold but of tinsel. The jewels too are fake. But not the ritual. A marriage ceremony has the makings of a fantasy—the bride in shimmering red, the groom riding a white horse, the baraat led by liveried musicians playing tin bands, the bidai, a parting laced with tears. Even a samoh lagan, a group marriage arranged to marry off poor Muslim girls in the courtyard of an ancient shrine, makes an effort to befit a time-worn tradition.

Guests amble past the dais seeking to see the faces of the brides hidden in ghungats. An elderly woman seated beside each bride diligently raises the girl's head, parts the veil, reveals the face for viewing. If marriages are made in heaven why do these brides look so desolate? I have yet to meet a happily married Muslim woman, I remark. 'Don't I look happy?' laughs Parizad, sitting amidst a circle of women who are dressed in brocades and decked in jewels like the brides on stage. Looking happy and being happy are two different things, I muse. Eyes turn still as she turns around. 'I will tell you my story when we meet someday,' she says disappearing in a crowd of chirping women.

So you are a happy woman, I ask Parizad when we meet the next day at an ice cream parlour. 'I was happier as a child, despite my father,' she says licking her favourite Chocolate Ripple cone. 'Everytime I laughed my father raged. Perhaps he hated me.'

There is no rancour in her voice as she recounts the tales of her father's cruelty. He would shut her in a small, dingy, room with a big black cat. He would throw her in a rose bush and enjoy seeing her enmeshed in thorns. Once he bit her cheek and left his teeth marks on it. And once he pushed her hand under the tap of a boiling samovar. 'He hated all his children and me the most,' says Parizad blankly. 'We were perhaps born of compulsion not love.'

One of twelve children, Parizad has tender memories of her mother. She remembers her as always pregnant. If there was one in the womb, another was holding on to her finger learning to walk. In an age when women observed strict purdah, her mother went to Tibbia College and studied to be an Unani doctor. In those days a wall with slits would separate the girls from the boys. Parizad's mother graduated with a degree in medicine and clad in a burqa led a delegation to demand that government jobs be created for women doctors, succeeding in getting one herself.

A full time job, a clinic in the house and twelve children kept her busy. 'Whatever she earned she would spend it on us, on fruits, clothes, our school books. Her main concern was that her children should be brought up well, should go to good English medium schools and learn to stand on their feet. She would go around to schools, bring admission forms and fill them up. But my father would refuse to sign and tear them up. Why should only a father have the right to sign for a child and not a mother, she would cry. My father perhaps resented her spirit, her diligence. He did nothing, went around in a Honda car. He was the pampered son of a rich man.'

Child of her mother, Parizad grew up to be a confident young woman. She was good in school and at home followed the ways of her mother. 'If I wanted a new night suit I would stitch it myself. I would embroider daisies on my handkerchiefs, and could brew a good pot of tea if a guest arrived.' Such qualities were considered assets in a well-groomed girl, raising her value in the marriage market. Women would come around and ask for her hand for a son or a nephew. 'You can get Rs 40,000 for your son. I won't even give four paise to my daughter. I am a mazdoorni, a worker,' her mother would say. Her father believed that a girl should be married when she turned fourteen. He pounced on a marriage proposal whilst her mother was on tour, announced it, had the cards printed. 'I became a spectator to my own marriage,' states Parizad. 'When my mother returned she could do nothing. I was married!'

She was wedded to a man she had not seen or known. On their wedding night he sat on the verandah and read a book. She sat in bed and cried. The next day they were packed off to Aurangabad for their honeymoon. 'You have five items to take care of,' said her brother-in-law at the station. 'Four bags and him.' She took charge of a man who was to remain a bundle throughout their married life. While young couples wandered around the temples of Ellora, Parizad sat in the guest house watching her husband reading a book. He would at times comment on a pretty sunset, a bird's song, then lapse back into silence. Read a book, he would advise, if she sought his attention. 'Am I not pretty, not worthy of him, I would wonder,' says Parizad remembering that agonizing time. 'He was a good man but he was never a companion. When I returned home to my mother I cried long in her arms. She realized that what had happened to her was happening to me.'

She was doomed to a marriage out of which there was no escape. Divorcing him would have meant budnaami, disgrace. Besides, there were two children to think of. Parizad was left with no choice but to stay and look after her husband, a sick man. He was given shocks and anti-depressants. 'When he was well he would realize what I was going through and say "I have tortured you". He allowed me to do what I wanted. But I never felt the love of a husband. I could not make any other male friend as I felt it was morally wrong. Men can't give that kind of friendship. They only want sex.'

Then, Parizad realized the spirit within her. She found the strength to laugh and talk as if she was happy. 'My spirit matured with each blow. I have gained maturity and learnt a great deal about life in these twenty years. I do not know if it is God or me. Does one's conviction and ability to fight come from religion? I am not sure. Most women who profess to be religious have no inner strength. They may pray five times a day and fast for thirty days during Ramzan. They do this not because they love God but because they fear society. Those who were religious like my sister-in-law had no compassion. They exulted in seeing me tortured, hid my husband's sickness from me . Confronting them made me strong. It is better to suffer and be strong than give up. Now my sons are my friends. I have a job that fulfils me. I have reconciled to my husband.'

Parizad is now the headmistress of a primary school where poor Muslim girls, their heads draped in square green scarves, come to study. It is an Islamic school which besides giving a regular education grooms girls in the tenets of their faith. 'If I was not religious I would not have got the job,' says Parizad. 'It is a challenge to meet the educational and administrative levels of the school.'

She too wears the green scarf on her head in keeping with the norms of the school. 'At first I felt hot and perspired. Now it is a habit, a discipline that gives a certain tone to life. I feel good seeing the fruits of my work—watching the children learn, the young girl teachers talk and express themselves. I have gained a respect which I never got at home.'

A year later, back in Hyderabad at a wedding again, I meet Parizad. Young women move, dressed in radiance, the strains of shehnai ring loud in an enclosed hall, in a corner sit a group of old women dressed in white. They are widows. Among them is Parizad her head closely draped in a colourless sari, her face without the glow, her eyes swollen. I do not recognize her. She smiles vaguely, comes up and hugs me. 'My husband is gone,' she weeps. The man with whom she spent twenty years, is no more. His death does not spell a release but reinforces a deeper tragedy. Doomed to the life of a widow means donning a mask of white, that separates her from the living. Will she marry again? I dare not ask. She sits still holding my hand, her eyes vacant. The women around us chirp. The band outside plays wedding songs.

Mahbubunissa

'I gave up purdah when my hair turned grey'

She stood among the racks of books, ran her fingers over them and cried. That was Mahbubunissa's first day at the college library. Her husband was dead and she had inherited his job. In his lifetime, she had not left the house alone and without a burqa. When she arrived wearing one she invited stares and comments. She was advised to give it up. A few times the girl who worked with her, hid it. *'Burqa ki towheen hogi*—I will not dishonour the veil. I will give it up myself when the time comes,' she told them. When her hair began turning grey, she knew the moment had arrived. 'When I noticed the first white hairs in my head I said, *bala talli,* the evil has passed. I stopped wearing the burqa. No one looks at an old woman.' That evil for which she does not mourn is her spent youth.

Widowed at twenty-two, Mahbubunissa's only security in a world of men, was the burqa. Like a black armour, it enclosed and protected her. Without it she would have felt vulnerable, less able to cope. Once within the college premises, she would remove the burqa and go to work. She learnt to read and write, paid a colleague forty rupees a month to teach her the alphabet. After sixteen years she can now read the numbers that identify books, can even read the names of the books and the authors. At first while replacing a book she would leave half the book out of the shelf, have someone check it and then put it back. She gained confidence with the years. Now, those who visit the library seek her help and she is able to give it. Starting with a salary of Rs 250 she has graduated to Rs 1500. She no longer cries in the racks, no longer finds herself isolated as the 'burqawali' on campus.

Born in a village, Mahbubunissa never went to school. Like all the Muslim girls in her village she was taught to recite suras from the Koran and do her daily namaz, Islami talim being the only education thought necessary for women. When she was married and came to live in the city her world remained within the home, centred around a husband and two children. When her husband died only the walls moved. Her mother-in-law gave her a room and charged her twenty rupees, previously the rent of her entire house.

'Those were difficult times,' recalls Mahbubunissa. And yet she bears no bitterness against her husband's family who kept her children starved when they returned from school. 'Even if there was chicken cooked in the house my children would not get it. I would return home to find them sitting in the dark. They were too small to switch on the lights.'

'On the way back from the college, I would stop at the market to pick up vegetables. I would come home, cook and feed them. My daughter helped to wash dishes, sweep the floor. My son sat under the street lamp studying. I have enrolled both of them in English-medium schools. I want my children to eat well, wear good clothes and study. What I do, does not matter.'

She has no time to say her prayers five times a day, she admits. She prays at dawn and riding the bus to work she counts her beads, her *La Illaha Illallah*, a thousand times. She tries to help her family, visits them regularly and shares in their dukh-sukh, their joys and sorrows. That's her religion. Her good actions she hopes will bring her children God's blessings. 'If I can bring up my children as good human beings I would be happy in this life,' she says simply. The fact that life and its joys have bypassed her, does not pain her. 'I have no desires left. They all died with my husband. All I have of his memory are these gold earrings. I will not sell them as they are his last souvenir. He had bought them with his last salary of twenty-six days.'

Sugra

'I won't wear purdah in America'

'I hear his voice and I can read his face,' says Sugra looking away. She has just received her monthly love letter from her fiancé who is an electrical engineer in the United States. She carries the audio-cassette around in her hand-bag, playing it again and again. She knows his voice better than his face. She never saw him when he came around to the house to see her. When his sisters dragged her into the drawing-room, she stood in front of him with eyes downcast. She fled in a flutter. He saw her, liked her and went away knowing that she would be his bride. When he gets leave from his job he will come back and take her away.

Meanwhile Sugra floats in a dream, listening to the sound of his words. He talks to her, sings her film songs, of love and longing. In answer, she sings back. 'It is better than writing letters,' she confides. 'Hearing the way he talks I can tell what kind of a man he is. I can feel his temperament. I know he is gentle and religious, just the way I am.'

Echoes of distant lands have begun to float in the enclosed courtyards of Sugra's neighbourhood. Girls who never stepped outside their homes have begun to travel to the Gulf countries, to the US and Canada. Muslim men who have migrated abroad always return to the old city looking for gentle brides, who are poor but from decent homes. Sugra is among them. Daughter of a postal clerk she grew up cloistered in a Muslim neighbourhood. In the twenty-two years of her life she has not been anywhere.

And yet the prospect of going to America does not frighten her. She will be travelling with her husband, she says. 'I have never gone alone outside the house. When I went to school I always wore the burqa. It protected me, gave me security. I wear it because of the mahaul, the environment, not because I like it. I won't wear it in America. People won't pass comments at me if I walk alone or bare-headed on the road. Here they do. At times it can be a disadvantage. A burqawali can be pushed around in a crowd. She has no identity.'

Sugra has grown up in Darul-Shifa, one of the oldest neighbourhoods in the city of Hyderabad where girls traditionally live within walls. And when they step out, they wear the burqa. 'I have always lived with Mummy-Papa,' she chirps. 'Whatever their life is, mine is too. It is a nice life, as nice as life can be in this part of the city. I do not know what life is like elsewhere. Girls here do not go around. If she is seen outside people say, is she a girl? Look how she wanders. When I was a child they used to say that girls can't do certain things. Why teach girls? they said. Why not? I would ask. I insisted on going to school. After matriculation I became a teacher in a kindergarten for they refused to let me go to college. Then I joined a technical training course. I want to learn. As I can't go out I learn from whatever I see around me. I have seen the museum. I have also been to Golconda Fort.

'In school I joined the NCC and went to a camp. I felt good when I was outdoors. I thought I was another person. What is freedom? Not just wandering here and there, but finding a position for yourself, being happy. It all depends on yourself, how you conduct yourself. I have great faith. I like my mazhab, my religion. My parents are deeply religious. They taught me what to do, how to behave in order to stay well in this world and in the next world. I feel good when I pray and uneasy when I don't. How can you live in this world, keep eating your meals three times a day and not pray? You don't live for this life alone but for the next. Yes, I believe in a heaven and a hell. Where exactly it is I don't know. If Allah wills he can create it, in any space. He can change a particle into a mountain. Nobody has seen Allah but I know He is there. He is a noor, a light. I think my religion is the best but perhaps I say this because I do not know any other.'

I meet Sugra in a small vocational school in the old city where burqa-clad young Muslim girls come to learn different skills—tailoring, screen-printing, biscuit-making, photography and computers. 'We want to stand on our feet,' they say. For some this training can turn out to be an asset, the instructor informs me. It becomes a substitute for dowry. When a girl has a certificate from a government training centre her value in the marriage market goes up. This can save her from the clutches of undesirable grooms, she hums. When the parents are very poor, girls are often sold off to older, often married men. Young Muslim girls who never went out are beginning to flock to these training centres. Their fathers and husbands are yielding to the pressure, the promise of money. Will earning money earn them their respect, break the shackles, bring more freedom? 'Time alone can tell,' says the headmistress of the school. 'Let us move step by step. We are still on the first step.'

'I had to struggle to come here,' says Sugra. Her parents had withdrawn her from college and were waiting for marriage proposals. What will I do at home? cried Sugra. She persisted with her father and succeeded. When she was called for the interview they let her go. 'We will see later what happens,' they said. And when she was selected they stopped her. Should she go or not go, they debated for fifteen days. How can you let a girl work? said her aunt. Won't the people say you are living off the girl? Sugra finally went. She works and she learns. Her parents let her keep her salary. She will use it to furnish her trousseau. 'I don't want to be a burden on my parents. They have already spent so much on my sisters' marriages. Having watched the problems that go with marriage rituals I never really wanted to marry. But then I would have been considered a landori, a good-for-nothing. Learning a trade is like owning a weapon. I can fight those wagging tongues. And soon I will go away. I will see the world. The Prophet had said that one should travel even as far as China in order to gain knowledge. I will be going the other way.'

Ameena

Ameena's Hyderabad is no longer mine. In my Hyderabad even a beggar woman would bend low in a gesture of salaam and stand quietly by the car — a greeting without the stretching out of the hand. She claimed a sense of izzat, an honour which in her mind was her heritage, a tradition prized equally by all Hyderabadis.

In Ameena's Hyderabad that tradition stands debased. That izzat which even a beggar claimed is now traded for money. Days in the old city are lived randomly, for appetite alone. Men have lost pride in themselves. And women are humiliated, sold for a price in the name of marriage. Ameena, a girl in her teens who protested against being married to an ageing Arab from the Gulf and was returned to her parents after a legal battle, is just the tip of the iceberg.

When I went looking for Ameena, it seemed that a once unified basti was now spilling into slums, its integrity diffused. Amidst slush and mud and stench brooded neighbourhoods without a sense of history or tradition, that had been raised in a hurry, jelled into ghettos by fear and insecurity.

In this new 'old city' cordoned off by poverty, live more than five lakh Muslims. Ameena's family is one among them. Before I reached her two-room tenement I walked into hovels where every other Muslim girl seemed like Ameena. A decade ago it would have been difficult if not impossible to meet young girls outside their homes. Today groups of them crowd the new centres, set up by the government in the bowels of the Muslim ghettos, to learn a trade and 'stand on their own feet.' In the aftermath of the 'Ameena affair' the government of India has aided the Andhra Pradesh Women's Cooperative Finance Corporation in setting up twenty-four centres in the old city to provide vocational training to girls between the ages of fifteen and twenty, an age when they are most vulnerable to mis-matched marriages.

Of the sixteen centres, run by non-governmental organisations, I visited two. The first had sixty-two girls learning tailoring and fashion designing and the second taught fifty-two young girls zari work. A dynamic Muslim woman, a social worker by instinct, uneducated in the modern sense, ran the centre for zari work in a brick tenement of a new slum. Around a large wooden frame young girls, their heads draped, sat bent crafting paisleys and flower buds in gold and silver threads. They looked like children but their eyes were without wonder. More than half were married, said the lady director of the centre. Will the Arab-affected girls raise their hands, she called out in Urdu. A dozen hands went up.

Afzal Begum was a pretty girl, diminutive in size, with large kohl-lined eyes that simply stared. Now sixteen she was married two years ago to a sixty-two-year-old Arab. 'He was to wed my older sister,' she stammered. 'But he did not like her. He said she was too short. He chose me.'

What did he look like? 'I don't know. I did not see him.' Why did she marry him? 'I thought if I was married, my other sisters will also have a chance.'

Afzal has six sisters and seven brothers. Her father is a qawwali singer. He performs wherever he is called. During the month of Muhurrum he does not sing. And there is no money in the house even for food. Her mother does not work outside the house. Nor do the brothers. The older ones loaf around the city, the others are too young to work. None of them have been to school. And six girls wait to be married.

So when the broker brought the proposal of a man from Saudi Arabia the father readily agreed. The man was rich, they were told. Afzal Begum was dressed in tinsel red clothes and married off hurriedly. What was it like being a bride? 'He took me to a room in the hotel,' she mumbles staring at her small henna-stained hands. And what did he do? She lowers her eyes, her lips tremble. 'Everything,' she mutters. She cried. She tried to stop him. He persisted. 'No, I did not like him,' she states flatly. He left a day later and never returned. Afzal Begum was married for a night. Will she marry again? No, she gestures with her head. 'I want to stand on my own feet.'

'I have written many letters to him but I have got no answer,' says Naseem who was deserted two months after being married. He too was an old man. 'They said he is from Saudi Arabia. That's the address he gave. But they say he now lives in Yemen.' Who brought him to her house? 'A dalal,' she says simply, a man none of them had known before. Such dalals go around the old city and are directed to houses where young girls live, waiting to be married. Naseem is one of nine sisters. Her father is a lorry driver. Her mother is blind. 'He saw me. I did not see him,' admits Naseem a thin, fair girl. She lived with him in a hotel for two months. Then he left. She was pregnant then. Now she has a child who has not seen her father. 'I want to work and look after my daughter. No, I will never marry again. The thought repels me.' Nor will Atiya, darker and sadder looking. She had lived with him in the dalal's house for six months. She liked him. He had gone away once and returned. He went a second time and never returned. She has no address for him. Nor does she know where the dalal is. He fled to Bombay. She too has a son. She hopes to have her own tailoring business and look after her family.

The story is the same, the agony identical. Most of these girls come from large families where daughters outnumber sons. Only the fathers work. They are mostly rickshaw pullers, vegetable or fruit vendors, pavement hawkers or auto drivers. Their income is less than 500 rupees a month. Young boys in the family are sent off to work and learn in scooter repair workshops where they earn a rupee a day. Young girls stay at home, do domestic work and wait for the first opportunity to get married. They are easy victims to Arab grooms who come looking for young girls from decent families and offer a high bride price. 'Most of these girls were abandoned,' says the director of the centre. 'Our training programme will convert them into income-generating members of the family. They will become assets instead of being treated as burdens.' Her centre alone, I am told, received 400 applications from young Muslim girls. They are being trained in tailoring, zari work, agarbatti making, typewriting, and a beautician's course. They are given a free nutritious lunch and a health check-up every fortnight. The training period is nine months at the end of which they will be given certificates. Those who wish to set up businesses will be helped with loans. 'They are children brought up in the mud,' says the director mournfully. 'None of them were brought up with love or care. They were not taught that they should eat with their right hand, that they should get up before elders and not talk whilst sitting. They have no training, no religion. Yet the girls are very responsive. They are eager to learn to stand on their feet.'

When I finally reached Ameena's two-room hutment I felt I already knew the scenario. I found myself in an empty space filled only by a crowd of female bodies — her slim, wide-eyed mother, her eight siblings of varying ages, from age two to sixteen, and the looming presence of her father who was out of the house. 'Her father does not like the girls to go out. He has no money to send them to the centres in a rickshaw. They dare not step out without his permission,' blurts out the mother, a simple, illiterate village woman. Sitting across from her, Ameena seems poised. She is dressed in what she describes herself as a 'maxi', a long dress with frills, 'imported,' adds the mother 'from the Gulf.' A discoloured dupatta is thrown over her shoulders. She sits sullenly, says little. Is she always so quiet? 'No, she bosses over her sisters,' giggles the mother. What is she learning? Ameena lets her mother answer. She produces a stack of notebooks and opens them the wrong way. In one is scribbled the English alphabet, in another the Hindi vowels. Three teachers, I am told, come to the house to teach her. Will she not prefer to go to the centre and learn a skill, with other girls? 'Her father won't let her go out,' repeats the mother. 'It is a question of his honour.' Can he read? 'He can write his signature,' mutters Ameena. Sixteen hundred young Muslim girls are learning because of her, I tell Ameena. She looks blank, says nothing. 'Ameena thinks she is a cut above the rest,' says the social worker as she escorts me out of the house. 'She wants to be able to read and write and become a big madam, the kind that come to visit her from Delhi.' Her family crowd around the door as I leave. As I turn back to wave I see all their anxious faces. The only one missing is Ameena.

Rashida

'My religion does not stop me seeking knowledge'

Rashida takes pride in being a daughter of Anderkote. Her home clings precariously to a craggy hill and looks as if it will topple down. Most homes in Anderkote give the same impression. Rugged, poised amid the hills of Ajmer, Anderkote remains hemmed in by fortress walls—no longer of valour and chivalry which one associates with its Rajput history, but by poverty and frustration.

Those who live here are Nais, Chamars and Muslims. The dirt, the slush and the stink that choke its paths are exterior to her being. Through the slits of her burqa she sees little when she steps out of her threshold. There was a time when women did not do even this. The fact that they have is a sign of hope.

'When I hear of a place or people from whom I can learn, I put on my burqa and run out,' beams Rashida as she sits amidst a group of women who gather every week at a welfare centre. Rashida is the youngest among them, just twenty and unmarried. The women talk about their homes, the problems of raising children who have known no school, of husbands who dominate, of elders who squabble.

Rashida has yet to experience such agony. It is knowledge alone that she seeks and doggedly pursues. 'I was so excited when I heard about the centre. I did not know Hindi and I decided that I will learn it here. In fifteen days I mastered the alphabet. When I would come here dressed up, people would remark: "Is she going to a college or just a welfare centre?" For me, it is bigger than a university. It gives me an opportunity to meet people, learn new things. I hate archaic ideas. I like the new.

'That doesn't mean that I have not seen the new even in the Holy Koran. All that one wants to know of the world is in the Book. But when you see and experience the world it only gets a confirmation. My religion does not stop me from seeking knowledge.' Her voice is commanding, her tone is that of an ustani, a teacher.

As she speaks, a hush falls over the circle of women. They watch her in fascination. An elderly woman murmurs, 'In my time, if we spoke like this, or spoke at all, we would have been doomed.'

'Yes, she makes sense. But that sense comes from the books she has read, not from the life she has lived. She has not yet begun living life,' adds another. She was married to a mentally deranged man for twenty years. Whilst he lived, she never spoke. After his death, she found her liberation. She stepped out of the house to earn a living; she sent three of her younger children to school, furnished their shelter and turned it into a home.

What would you do if you were married to the wrong man? I ask Rashida.

'I would talk to him, argue with him and make him understand my viewpoint. If he listened to me, I would become his slave. If he didn't, I would persist until I changed him. If he were to irritate me, I would do the same. But if he continued to ill-treat me, I would leave him. It is better to go away rather than live a life of humiliation. Women must have self-esteem, then open their lips and go forward. If Allah has given life to everyone, doesn't a woman too have a right to live it her way? Where is it written that man should roam around and keep a woman locked? Where is it written that he should beat her into silence? God has made us equal. He has given us hands. If a man can go out and earn, can't a woman sit at home and earn too?'

Like most of the women who live in cloistered homes in Anderkote, Rashida works wonders with needle and thread. She embroiders, sews and crafts garments in gold thread. If a man earns Rs 200 as a tailor in Anderkote, a woman at home earns an equal amount.

'If you walk the right path, some day you will find your reward,' Rashida's mother would advise.

That faith, instilled so deeply in childhood, remains Rashida's guiding light. She not only recites the Koran daily as her mother taught her but reflects on it. 'If there is a lot of food in front of you, and you try to eat it all, you can't digest it. I do a little, and I am not afraid,' she asserts. 'There is no such thing as fear. We create it in our heads. Why be afraid of the ghosts and the dark? Just put on a light and they go away.

'I have understood that whatever God has helped me learn, I should share it with others. Namaz has strengthened my feelings, fortified my desires. I want to live and distribute my knowledge. It disturbs me to see how distant Muslims are from true faith, how backward they have become. Anyone who is alive and has the determination to learn and earn is not a sick person. If he lacks this drive, he is sick though he may claim to be living. Whatever I know—like keeping a good house, showing respect to elders, being confident in myself—I try to teach other women. I am thirsty for learning and I will distribute it as I get it.'

Royal Mothers Royal Daughters

'Religion and life bear an intimate connection'

In the heart of every Muslim woman in Bhopal survives a magical island. She traces it back to a vision, of four women who ruled and guided the destinies of the state for more than a hundred years. They ruled like men, rode horses and elephants, wore no veil and were referred to as Nawabs. In today's Bhopal, a city that has moved like any other, their memories live on, striking echoes in the daily lives of people. To meet a woman carrying the name Salma Sultan or Syeda Sultan is commonplace. The name is her own, not an appendage granted by a husband or a father. That's the way the queens were known, by their own names.

Bhopal's female lineage is traced back to the early years of the nineteenth century when Sarkar Qudsia Begum inherited the mantle of kingship on the death of her husband. She ascended the throne without a veil. To announce her abdication of the veil she held a formal ceremony to which she invited her male colleagues, the Prime Minister, the Commander-in-Chief and the Chief of her stable. He had taught her to ride. A passionate rider she loved horses and elephants. Like the legendary Haroun-al-Rashid, she would roam the streets of her city in a palanquin that had no curtains. She would sit under a tree in the common grounds and meet people, eat with them and listen to their problems. The tales of her wisdom and generosity remain part of the city's lore.

Traditions that began in her time were continued by her daughter Sikander Jehan Begum who too refused to wear the veil. The story goes that when an angry husband inflicted a sword wound on her she had it mended with four stitches and withdrew into the fort of Islamnagar from where she continued to rule.

Photographs show her standing fearless, dressed in the manner of men, a scarf tied over her head, a band aglitter with badges flung across her chest. Like her mother, she left no male heir but a daughter, Shah Jehan Begum, who ruled the state for thirty years. Scholar, author and builder she raised monuments that remain alive to this day. Among them is the impressive Tajul Masajid that she raised with her own private money.

Shah Jehan Begum's daughter Sultan Jehan Begum was as much a pioneer, in the educational field. She introduced free primary education, initiated reforms for women and children and wrote books herself. When she abdicated in favour of Nawab Hamidullah, the first male to rule the state after a hundred years, the patterns set by the queens had taken root. The mosques they raised had special areas where women could pray, where marriages could be solemnized and langars held to feed the poor. Schools and colleges opened their doors to women. Even the army was commanded to enrol women in its ranks. Court orders that in the male tradition were called Ata-e-Chobe were changed to the feminine Ate-e-Chobeena. Islam as a way of life was reflected in the affairs of government.

*

I am seated on the cold marble terrace of Tajul Masajid that was built by the grand Shah Jehan Begum. One of Islam's most acclaimed architectural marvels, it is as alive today as it was in the queen's time—not with the sound of prayer alone but with the chorus of tiny voices chanting the Holy Koran. Under the mosque's great roof, amidst the stone columns, on frail wooden benches, sit boys, their heads covered by round white caps, reciting the suras, moving their bodies in a rhythmic pageant. Religion remains integral to the daily life of Bhopal. All the mosques are filled to capacity on Fridays. In the mornings several of them turn their spacious premises into madrasas, religious schools, to instruct children about the Word of God. Tajul Masajid has a library, a hostel for boys, and a dining room to provide free meals to the 700 young boys who are enrolled in its school.

How well does a religious education equip these young people to go out and face a world far more complex than that of their parents? 'We Muslims of course need doctors, engineers, mechanics,' says a strident young male teacher. 'But we need these boys as much. Those who come to study deen, religion, here are not the sons of the rich but the children of farmers and workers who find themselves better equipped with what we teach. We get hundreds of letters from all over the country asking for maulvis and alims, teachers and scholars, to run schools according to our faith. They may not earn much but they stay alive. If these boys were to go to Aligarh University and get degrees, start wearing pants and shirts, it will seem like a crow trying to move like a swan. In practice deen and modernity do not mix though we say that they should. All we can give these children is a key to the treasure. It is for them to go out and discover it, make it relevant to their needs.'

To keep the mosques in good condition, tradition demanded that they be kept alive with prayer and learning. 'Religion and life bear an intimate connection,' says Kaiser Biya, a soft-spoken aristocrat who traces her lineage to a royal line that claims close links with the ruling families of Afghanistan. The martial Pathans who dominated Bhopal carried the tribal tradition of candour and directness in their relationships with men and with their God. Simple and God-fearing, a Pathan would do his ablutions with the mud of the earth, if he was digging it. And he would pray anywhere if it was the hour of prayer. 'Our Islam does not encourage ritual,' says Kaiser. 'We stress its pristine quality, its practical side. Islam means peace. It also means jehad, war against iconoclastic beliefs. Where the two meet lies the challenge of balance and of moderation, one that each of us has to work out. To make concessions for peace is the way of Islam.'

Kaiser Biya's voice is drowned by the voices of muezzins ringing out the afternoon azaan on microphones. Traditions, religious and secular, rooted in a royal past linger tenaciously. In many Muslim homes the portrait of the last Nawab, who acceded to the Indian Union in 1950, hangs on the wall. He is remembered as a Haji, who fulfilled his pilgrimage. Despite a western education he remained pious, reciting his suras before every meal; unlike his princely contemporaries he maintained no harem for women. His daughter Begum Sajida Sultan learned to hunt and fly a plane, had a collection of guns and rifles, and presided over the women's hockey association. He lived in a palace that had neither opulence nor feudal decadence. Everyone ate together and observed a decorum that lacked servility and the exaggerated courtly manner. The qualities that filtered down from the Nawabs to the nobility, then to the common man continue to be visible in changing Bhopal. Then, people lived in mud houses, cooked their bread on firewood and prayed in the mosques across the road. Today in their homes sit television sets and VCRs but the essence of the past still lingers. This is so, despite the fact that the standard of living is higher and the spirit of competition is threatening to become a way of life even among Muslims. If a family is watching a film on television and the sound of the azaan rings out, they may switch off the sound out of deference but not the image on the screen, I am told. The women though are more religious than the men, they remain dominant in the house, carry their own names and their own identity. They may not be aware of it, but do it naturally. The birth of a girl child is not frowned upon in Pathan families. A Pathan, in the true spirit of Islam, gives no dowry, instead he pays money when he takes the bride home. Some of that spirit is reinforced in the recent tale of a girl who chased away the groom's party when they demanded a scooter as part of her dowry.

'I do believe every Muslim girl in Bhopal holds her own as an individual,' says one young niece of the former Nawab. 'They understand the rights given to them by Islam; they do not accept them because they are forced upon them. Though my mother met the viceroy wearing her veil, purdah was never very strict in Bhopal. My father was a deeply religious man but he was equally enlightened. Islam was not a drill for us. Islamiyat does not mean to me following dictates, praying five times a day, wearing a veil. I ask my own heart and follow it. If I get a call from within I stand up and pray. I won't take a drink before an old aunt out of respect. But if I am with a fanatic I will drink out of vengeance. To be honest, not to hurt anyone and to be a good human being, is my Islam.'

She went to a convent and studied with Christian nuns. Christmas, she remembers, was as much a festival in their home when her father who never drank alcohol would sprinkle brandy on the Christmas pudding to bring cheer. Hers has been an urbane education as is her way of life. True to her life style, she dresses the modern way, enjoys her vodka spiked with green chillies after sundown and spends the best part of her day working in her own garment factory that is located in part of the family's sprawling mansion. 'I want to be on my own,' she asserts as her husband sits in the shadows of the evening, reading a book, nursing his Scotch in a tall crystal glass.

The same hour, in Sajida Biya's home, is a time for prayer. The maghrib azaan, the call for prayer at sunset, fills the lane and floats into her home. As I enter the dimly lit apartment I see her getting ready for namaz, wrapping herself in a dupatta. My entrance does not deter her. She asks me to wait while she stands to pray along with Amma, her maid servant for thirty years. 'My mother never missed a single day's namaz,' she says, her head draped, her face fervent. 'Namaz is part of my nature. I learnt to pray as if it was play. My mother never gave the impression that it was a drill. When she wanted the children to count the tazbi, the beads which when counted carry vibrations direct to heaven, she had them made for us. We recited the name of Allah a hundred times before going to bed, that's how we children learnt. That's the way Islam is. It is fitri deen, a natural faith.'

A woman of fifty, Sajida is a spinster. The man she was to wed married someone else. 'That hurt me,' she mumbles. 'No, not because I was in love with him. But because I was married to him in my mind. As my mother would say the word given among people who are decent and God-fearing itself amounts to marriage. Yet, my inner voice told me to stay unmarried—it was God's command.' She stayed many years with her mother. 'She was my only dream, the most pious woman I have known. Her silence and her courage were exemplary. She became a widow as a young woman and struggled hard to bring us up. Only after her death did I come to realize what it is to be alone. Life stood before me menacing like a mountain that threatened. I faced it with the strength that she had given me as a child.'

Sajida lives with her old maid in a basement apartment, in

part of a sprawling mansion that once belonged to her family. It used to be the Nawab's naqar-khana from where the drums rang at official ceremonies. The house lies in ruins today as a legal battle for its ownership rages in the civil court. 'Can you imagine me standing in a court?' she asks. 'We never observed purdah in our family. But that does not mean we can walk on the street bareheaded. I am a great believer in khandaan, in a person's ancestry, and breeding. It is that which gives me confidence and it is faith that gives me strength. I pray that my heart stays clean, that when I call Allah! I get an answer back, even a small one.'

There are many like her in the old city, whose faith keeps them alive. It is that which gave them the strength to face a tragedy of the proportions of the Bhopal gas leak, which devastated the city. People formed groups to help others out at the cost of their own lives. 'I have eaten gas myself,' says Sajida as if she is talking about someone else. 'I awoke with a pain in my throat, my mouth was bitter and I could not figure it out. I began praying. I recited the kalma twice, then could not. Oh God, I cried, make my dying easy. Then my neighbours came and we all went out together. I was giddy watching such tall men and strong women collapsing. Thousands died. No one knew who was Muslim and who was Hindu. Everywhere there were mass graves and cremations. When such a tragedy happens one wonders—is it God's way of testing our strength?'

Najma

'Women were never barred from the mosque, only exempted'

To this city enlightened by the wisdom of far-sighted queens Najma Heptullah owes her beginnings. Child of Bhopal, grand-niece of Maulana Abul Kalam Azad, the illustrious scholar and national leader who fought for India's freedom along with Gandhi and Nehru, Najma presides as deputy chairman of the Rajya Sabha. She traces her roots to the Islam of Mecca from where her ancestors migrated to India giving to the country of their adoption the best of their dedication. They first settled in Calcutta, then moved to Bombay and finally Bhopal.

Her grandmother, sister of Azad, was inspectress of schools during the reign of Sultan Jehan Begum who stressed progress for women in all fields particularly education. In her time parents were paid to educate daughters. While the men often lagged behind, busy with sport and shikar, the women studied, joined services and looked after the house. Every house boasted at least one woman graduate.

'For a woman to be educated in Bhopal was not an exception but the rule,' says Najma. Like many girls of her generation she too went to Sultania College in a special bus that would stop in the college portico which was screened by sheets.

'We observed purdah but it did not deter us,' claims Najma. 'My grandmother wore the burqa and travelled all over the country. So did my aunt who was a teacher of Urdu in college, a poet who was intensely aware of the world around her. The atmosphere in our house was deeply religious. That is precisely the reason why so much stress was laid on our education. We had the right understanding of the Islamic credo. If I was not educated I would not be sitting in the Parliament today with such dignity and honour.'

Islam, explains Najma, lays great emphasis on ilm and talim, on knowledge and education. 'The Prophet had said travel as far as China for the sake of learning. And he did not mean only Dini-ilm but Dunyavi-ilm, not just knowledge of one's own faith but also that of the world. Islam is a way of life and knowledge is an integral part of it.

'How can you be a hakim if you do not know the nature of plants, herbs and roots? How can you educate a child if you are an illiterate mother? In our family the women were as educated as the men. Maulana Azad's father, a great religious scholar who studied at the universities of Al Azhar and Istanbul, educated his daughters in the same manner as he did his son. The Koran was enshrined in their hearts a hundred years ago.'

To this day Maulana Azad's *Tarjuman-ul-Quran* remains the most classic interpretation of the Holy Book. In its preface, written in 1930 in the cell of Meerut's District Jail, Azad reflects on the deterioration in the scholar's approach to the meaning of the Koran. 'It is a result of the gradual decadence in the quality of the Muslim mind itself,' he writes. 'When the commentators found that they could not rise to the heights of the Koranic thought they strove to bring it down to the level of their own mind.'

'I was brought up to pray but also told the meaning of prayer,' says Najma. Her mother's father would sit with the children every night after dinner and talk to them about namaz, roza, the essentials of religion. To do wazu, to wash oneself before prayer meant paying great attention to personal cleanliness. In the desert where there was a dearth of water, the Prophet instructed that wazu should be done five times a day before each namaz. The ritual of washing was elaborate but every part of it has a meaning. As did fasting in Ramzan. It disciplined the system, made a person aware how it felt not to eat, understand hunger and thirst. 'If your stomach is full how will you understand another's hunger?' asks Najma. 'When I fast I know its importance. Same thing with prayer. It is bowing before God, knowing that you are answerable to Him, knowing that He sees you all the time, even when you are in a closed room.'

Islam, she explains, is a community religion. The Prophet asked men to go to the mosque five times a day and pray. Prayer is like a drill. You follow the instruction of one man in the mosque, stand in a line in a manner that the foot of one touches the foot of the other, and there is no high or low, black or white in a congregation. At the end of the namaz you turn to the right and greet the man next to you with *As-salamu-alaikum* then turn to the left. That gives an opportunity to acquaint oneself with the other, know men in his neighbourhood, find out who is sick or dead, if a guest has arrived, if there is a marriage or a function taking place.

Much in the same way Haj brings people of the world together. The Prophet would apply attar and instruct men not to eat garlic or onion when going to the mosque lest the odour offended others. These, says Najma, are the beauties of Islam, the attention that is given to small things that make the texture of our daily life. It is the youngest and the most modern religion. At a time when women were buried alive the Prophet gave equality, honour and rights to women. A woman was entitled to own, inherit, and sell property. She had the right to choose whom she wanted to marry. Of course, with these rights were tied obligations. If they were not respected that was another matter. It is not the mistake of religion, believes Najma, but of men. 'We live in a man's world where men make rules. Women were never barred from going to the mosque. They were only exempted as they had household chores. When they go to Haj or Umra they go and pray in the mosque.'

Tayeba Begum

'It is He who controls the moon and man who walks on it'

To Tayeba Begum's school in Bhopal veiled women come to learn and seek. Its roof overlooks the minarets of Tajul Masajid and Jama Masjid and reaffirms and reassures the spirit of those who seek. Down below, encircling a green courtyard, is the madrasa, a school for which Tayeba Begum single-handedly raised money. She made plans for its building despite constant resistance. 'Your school won't be built as long as I am alive,' said one man to whom she went seeking a water connection. 'The school will be built,' Tayeba Begum told him. 'It will be built while you are alive. And if you don't help and give us water, you will die.' He lived to see it built. 'I feel I have been blessed,' says Tayeba Begum, her face radiant. The dark shadows, inflicted by two broken marriages, have receded. 'If I did not have this work, perhaps my past life would have remained a burden,' she says. 'God destined that I do this work.'

She does not dwell on her personal life but talks at length about her commitment, to spread the deen, the religion of her Book. 'My life? It is not much to talk about. It is short and simple. My first marriage lasted for two years. Also the second. All it gave me was a still-born baby. Love? That is a supreme emotion. I did not even get the courtesy that any normal relationship commands.'

To the madrasa is tied her mission. Her relaxation comes from being with children and the plants that she nurtures on her roof. She prunes them, waters them and exults in watching a bud turn into a bloom. 'See the earth, the myriad colours in each of my rose bushes. I put the same water, the same soil in each of them. Why then do they bloom in all these hues? Isn't there a force that designs this nizam-e-kayenat, the governance of this universe? Don't they reveal the nature and quality of God?' She has understood her Allah and realized His presence, in her life and in the world. And this, she explains, stems not from books that she has read but from the experience of having lived.

Being born in a religious family did not prevent Tayeba Begum from going to college to study medicine. She saw the wonder of God in human chemistry and wondered why He had disappeared from the minds of scientists. 'They may have gained knowledge but not the control over it,' she says. 'Only God has that control. It is He who controls the moon and man who goes to walk on it. One who is disappointed in God is a kafir, non-believer.'

Why always such fear of God? I ask her. She explains, with an example: 'If you have a beautiful piece of silk and you want it made into a dress you go to a tailor who you feel can be trusted to do a good job. While the tailor cuts the cloth and sews it he has a sense of fear that if he makes a mistake you will lose faith in him. It is a fear born out of regard and consideration. Even whilst the Prophet was praying all night he worried. "Have I done my prayers right? Did I err anywhere that goes against the majesty of God?" When such fears, born of love, crowded his mind, he asked for God's forgiveness. That is the bond of man with God. If you live life according to the ways He willed for you, following the Prophet, then your whole life becomes a prayer.'

She is a teacher whose way is simple but persuasive. In 1947, the year of Partition, she decided to take up the teaching of Islam. 'When I saw the destruction of my community I was deeply pained. I wondered whether we had become less faithful. I wanted to make the Muslims come back to a true deen so that they could deserve God's help.' What about the women who come to learn religion in her school? How well do they practise what they learn? 'They don't live Islam because of the environment they live in,' she explains. 'But young people today, more than they did in my time, are joining tableegh, travelling for forty days on trips in the countryside to spread the teachings of Islam.'

Even more women today wear scarves on their heads and try to follow the code of conduct. Purdah is legitimate but can also become illegitimate. The way men have shuttered the women in purdah is illegitimate according to her. To deny the existence of woman is not Islamic. Women in the Prophet's time even went into battle. 'When our men isolate women, divorce them without reason they are going against the spirit of Islam. It is backwardness, not knowledge. Praying five times a day alone is not Islam. Without work and labour you can't walk the path of Islam. To hurt another's sentiment is a sin. If you run down another's God, they will run yours down too. Islam means to accept, to admit. Even when a kafir called on the Prophet he would be met with courtesy. Akhlaaq, an exemplary disposition and good manners, is the cornerstone of Islam. The Prophet would sit in the mosque with his head turned in a particular direction. When asked why, he said "From that direction comes a good breeze, where good things are being discussed by good people." To learn is as important in Islam as it is to pray and seek.'

But what about those who seek and are not Muslims? Doesn't God rest in them too? Isn't He Rab-ul-alameen, God of the universe? 'Yes, He is,' she says, casting her long gaze towards a vivid blue sky that spans her open roof. 'To search is man's nature. Even the man who worships an icon which he has crafted with his own hands nurses the same fervour. Didn't Abraham come out of the cave driven by the same search? He looked at the star and exclaimed, "That must be my Rab, my Lord." When the moon rose he cried again, "This is my Rab." And when the moon sank and the sun rose, bigger than the moon, Abraham said, "This is my Rab." Each one seeks God in his own way. When you recognize Him, then the desire to live according to His wishes is born in you and a purer life becomes possible. In the journey of life some lids are banged, some veils descend and we lose our focus and stray. But if the search remains, we always return to His sanctuary....'

Gulbaden's Daughter

'A sanctuary that gives her freedom'

Like the shrine she remains unchanged. I do not know her name. I have watched her through the years in Sur Towk ka Alawa, a reliquary in old Hyderabad, that preserves the relic and memory of Imam Zainul-Abedin, the only son of Imam Husain who survived the tragedy of Karbala. Like the shrine she remains unchanged. A woman in her middle years with tired black eyes, a small lean body and a face which like a mask seems to guard a secret. She greets each visitor to the alawa with a deep salaam, a gesture that seems more a habit with her than a ritual courtesy. She asks no questions, shows little interest in the private lives of those who come to pray and seek. Unlike the moon-faced flower vendor, who smiles and chats with visitors while his small deft fingers string sehras of jasmines and roses, flowery veils that are traditionally tied over the faces of brides and grooms, but in the alawas are offered to alams, insignia of the imams.

In Sur Towk ka Alawa sits the alam of the fourth imam commanding the presence of a deity. The story goes that it preserves a remnant of the towk, the iron armour that the imam had worn when he was taken prisoner and dragged under its weight from Karbala to Damascus. The alawa that draws its name from the alam dates back to Qutub Shahi times when in its premises was housed the Durul-Shifa, an Unani hospital. It was felt that the presence of the alam would invoke its blessings for the sick. The king of that time appointed a caretaker for the alawa.

That sixteenth century tradition has passed on to the nameless woman who continues to take care of the alam. She lives in the alawa and receives for her tasks a hadiya, a small amount of money from the dusty coffers of the young prince whose grandfather, the last reigning Nizam of Hyderabad, was a devout Shia supporting the shrines and mosques in the old city. The alawa preserves the spirit of his time though he is no more.

Come Muhurrum, the alawa ritually returns to life. Its walls are painted green, its floors covered with long white sheets, its air recharged with incense. Women in black chadars and men in black sherwanis enter through separate entrances to gather in halls partitioned by curtains. They chant nauhas, hymns commemorating the martyred imams, and weep as if it is a necessary part of the ritual. Like the women, men bring sehras for the alam, cling to it weakly and pray. Prayer is to attend. The woman in the shrine stands beside the alam as if in attendance. For years that has been her role, giving strength in sorrow, heart in celebration.

One quiet month when I arrive on a ritual visit I find the alawa deserted. Black goats reminiscent of shepherd prophets browse in the courtyard. The flower vendor is away. Small and shrivelled, the woman sits coiled on a tattered prayer rug, her weary face turned heavenward, towards a faded print of the Kabah hung high on a western wall. Unaware of my presence, she remains in sajda, bowed to the ground for what seems a very long time. I wait as the sun declines and shadows lengthen in the empty courtyard. Within minutes the pageant changes.

A procession of men, dressed in black, enter the alawa carrying a coffin on their shoulders. It is covered with a black cloth, strewn with red roses. Beating their chests, chanting a hymn in elegiac rhythm, they make a circle around the alawa and place the coffin in the courtyard to invoke the blessings of the alam. I wonder who has died. 'He must have been a young man,' says the woman rolling up the prayer rug. 'For they are chanting an elegy of Ali Akbar, the young son of Imam Husain who died in the battle of Karbala.' Funerals such as these pass by every other day. She watches them with eyes glazed. 'You lose a son, a fortune, a house. We forget the loss, even the memory fades. But not the sorrow of Husain and his family. That tragedy is always fresh.' The story of Karbala, repeated for hundreds of years, continues to evoke the deepest feelings, transcending daily human tragedies.

What about her own life, I wonder? Did she have a son? Was she married? Did she have a family? 'It's a long story,' says a woman visitor leading me into the courtyard. She too has watched the woman for many years. 'They say her father was a Nawab.' She pauses, adjusts her dupatta over her head and continues in a conspiratorial tone. 'Her mother was a maid in a noble mansion. Drawn to her looks the Nawab named her Gulbaden and made her his casual wife. Slave girls in those days carried such euphonic names, as would please the ears of their masters. Gulbaden had a daughter. When the Nawab died she was chased out of his house. She had no family, no money, no roof over her head and nowhere to go. With the girl she arrived on a winter night in the alawa where she found shelter and stayed on. She did not take to the streets as many women tend to do when they are abandoned. In the circle of the alawa she found her protection, a job to do. She cared for the alam for ten long years with a faith that was unmatched. When she died of tuberculosis her daughter, already a woman, took over. She has gone the mother's way. She too, they say, married and was deceived. Some say she even had a child. God knows where it is. We have only seen her. She remains thin like a bamboo, never changes. She prays for hours, she cleans the alawa, sweeps the courtyard, feeds the goats and sits alone praying deep into the night. Only God knows her prayer.'

Centuries ago, in another part of the Muslim world, one other woman had lived such a life in the presence of God. She was Lalla Mimouna, an Algerian peasant woman who could neither read nor understand the Koran. 'Mimouna knows God and God knows Mimouna' was the prayer she had invented for herself. That attention remains the nature of prayer for many women who seek to live invisibly. The nameless woman in the shrine strives to live in that sublime tradition. In the service of the alam she has not only found her God but a refuge. Perhaps even a freedom . . . .

Mehdi Begum

'I took the name of Allah as my child lay dying'

Mehdi Begum's young daughter died during the curfew, that was imposed in old Hyderabad during the communal riots. She had a fever and the family could get no doctor or medicine for her. The shops were closed. All access to the outside world was banned. No one was quite sure when the child died. She was buried quietly at night. A daytime funeral, the police warned, would arouse further communal passions. Mehdi Begum wrapped her in an old white sheet as there was no shroud. The father carried her in his arms and buried her under a tree. There were no mourners. And there was no incense to burn. A child's funeral was robbed of even fragrance. And a family denied a dignified mourning.

Mehdi Begum lives in the shadow of Bi-ka-alawa, a sacred shrine dedicated to Prophet Mohammed's daughter, Fatima. The Bi-ka-alam installed in the shrine is a relic made of thick wood which, according to legend, was part of the takht on which Bi was given the ritual bath after her death. To her alam is tied the faith and belief of generations of Shias who live in Hyderabad.

The Bi-ka-alam is installed on the night of the new moon that signals the coming of Muhurrum, the New Year and the month of mourning for the martyrs of Karbala. On the tenth of the month, the day when Bibi's beloved son Husain was killed in the battle of Karbala, thousands wait to see the alam. Like a grand personage, the alam is taken out in a procession, seated on an elephant that ritually sheds tears like the men and women dressed in black, who beat their chests, chant dirges and mourn. It is a moment of sublime grief publicly shared. The nagaras, the ancient drums at the gate of the shrine, are turned upside down, as they are on the death of kings.

Mehdi Begum, a child of this faith, deems it a blessing to live in the shadow of the shrine. But there is no air of sanctity about this neighbourhood that links its destiny to a symbol some hundred years old. To reach Mehdi Begum's home I travel through a maze of identical lanes that knit a constricted world. A relentless sun beats overhead. Dust blows in the hot breeze, mangy dogs sleep in doorways, children play lethargically with pebbles, crows feast on the garbage that is littered everywhere. A heavy sack curtain hangs over the entrance door to Mehdi Begum's home. She sees it as a defender of her privacy and respectability. It helps veil her poverty from the outside world. Such curtains hang on many doors in the Muslim quarters of the old city. They come as part of a young woman's dowry.

In the adab—etiquette—of the old city I pause outside the curtain, clap my hands and announce my arrival. A boy peeps out, withdraws, and emerges again with a hesitant smile. Holding aside the curtain, too heavy for his small hands, he lets me in. I find myself in a dingy space that serves as the washroom. A bucket tumbles, a few vessels crash at my feet before I enter the space where Mehdi Begum is standing to welcome me. 'Aayee, aayee,' she says with old-world courtesy. 'Please sit down.' From a corner she pulls out the rusty metal chair reserved for an occasional guest. I prefer the farsh, a white sheet spread out on the ground and arranged with round bolsters. The farsh fills her room and is obviously used for sitting, eating, sleeping. The only other objects that suggest any utility or comfort are a small table fan placed on a stool; a cassette player, a glass vase stuffed with plastic flowers; and, nailed to a wall, a wooden shelf filled with cassettes.

'The light has gone out,' she says even as she gets up in a reflex motion to put it on. 'Most of the time it is out. We are used to living in the darkness.' Near the roof, I notice a small opening which too has been curtained off with a piece of cloth. Why not let the sun come in, I suggest, looking at the hole. 'Cold air comes in,' she mutters, extending her hand to switch on the table fan. She would rather breathe the stale air scattered by a fan than risk the fresh air. As we sit in the semi-gloom trying to decipher each other, the bare bulb hanging from the roof sputters back to life.

In its sickly yellow light I see her pale olive face with large black eyes reddened by the strain of tears. In her twenties Mehdi Begum has the look of a tired woman. 'I was married at sixteen and had three children,' she says. 'The girl who died during the curfew was my first child.' I see the other two — the boy who sits clutching her sari, staring blankly as if in a daze, and a baby lying shrivelled on the farsh like a rag doll. There is nothing human about it. It neither moves nor cries. It, too, will perhaps perish for lack of sun and air, I morbidly tell myself. On the wall hang pictures of the dead girl dressed in party clothes. How did she die? I ask, staring at the child beaming out of a metal frame. 'Just a fever,' she says. 'She was sick for ten days while the curfew was on. We could not take her to the hospital nor get medicine, not even milk. My husband was unable to go to work. And there was no money in the house. When I counted the paisas I had saved it amounted to two rupees. We finally managed to get half a packet of milk and fed her. All the time I was praying and blowing my breath in the water I was giving her. The best medicine of the poor is prayer. But mine did not work. Did I falter in my faith? On the night my girl died I fumbled as I prayed and the thread that I had rubbed against the Bi-ka-alam to tie on her wrist, fell on the ground. Was it a sign telling me something?'

Questions such as these nag Mehdi Begum as she sits staring at the still baby on the floor. Death has nothing to do with such fears, I want to tell her. But I don't, for I have come to condole not trample on a belief that cements her fragile life. Let the baby get more sun and air and it will live, I say, determined to make her understand that sun and air besides babies are also gifts from God. 'It is difficult to find a house with a courtyard which is cheap and near the alawa,' she answers. She will not venture out of this charmed circle and move to another neighbourhood. She harks back to her imaan and that of her dead daughter. 'She took the name of Allah at every step,' she goes on, her voice lit with pride. 'Allah was on her lips when she woke up, when she went to sleep, when she ate her food. Did God take her away because

He loved her too? As she lay in my arms dying I also cried out to Allah. But my cry never reached Him. My door was closed. The policeman on duty knocked and hushed me back to silence. The curfew was on, he warned.'

Why was the curfew on? What brought about the killings, the riots, the communal fires? Who was responsible — the politicians, the mullahs or her neighbours? Such questions do not concern Mehdi Begum. 'It was the will of Allah.' A simple statement heavy with years of belief. She blames no one. Her immediate worry is how long it will be before her husband would be able to return to his shed in the park and resume his work of repairing cycle rickshaws. And would her young boy go back to school where he is enrolled in the first grade? Mehdi Begum never went to school. Nor was she taught how to read and write. But she learnt to recite the hymns and elegies written by her grandfather in praise of the martyrs of Karbala. She belongs to the long tradition of women who lived the spirit of poetry without an education.

Unaware of it in herself, she takes a quiet pride in her lineage and displays it on her wooden shelf. A small sepia photograph of an old man occupies a place of eminence next to the vase of plastic flowers. It is a kindly face with sad grey eyes. She neither has his eyes nor the faraway look that probes the wider arc of human anguish. Hymns that he wrote inspire her, help her to see personal tragedy in perspective. 'As my child was dying I was chanting the elegy my grandfather wrote about the death of the young daughter of Imam Husain, Sakeena who after her father's death was dragged to a prison and left alone to languish and die. My daughter's death pales in comparison.' Azadari, mourning in the memory of the martyred imams, for generations has provided women like Mehdi Begum a release and lent their grief a focus.

Jilani Bano

'A Muslim woman is an easy victim'

'Religion gives. It does not take,' says Jilani. 'It gives us the strength to live, to know the world, our own family and children. It gives us a framework, a discipline, a viewpoint.' Jilani is a writer. It was her father, an Islamic scholar, who passed on his tradition of knowing and questioning to her. Neither rigid nor short-sighted he loved music, drama and poetry and educated all his seven children. Her mother, a creature of a cloistered home who was married at thirteen, took pride in the fact that no woman in her family had married outside the clan for seven generations. 'Though wide apart in their thinking they lived together for sixty years,' remembers Jilani. 'If one did not have a meal, the other worried. They thought together on all issues that involved the family. My mother did not stop us from going to school, even the girls. She did not however approve of us learning to sing or paint. Later when I started writing she did not appreciate my writing stories and attending writers' meetings or conferences. I did not want to make my mother unhappy so I did not insist on doing things that she did not approve. I preferred to suppress my own wishes. So I was in a kind of purdah. Sharam and haya, to be reticent and private, are qualities drilled into every Muslim girl since she is a child. My father who understood the injunctions of the Koran would point out the false interpretations. Wearing a chadar that covers your body leaving your hands and feet free is the Islamic purdah, he would tell us. Not the burqa that like a tent encloses and inhibits. When I got married, a man of my own choice, I came out of purdah. My husband lends me support, shares my viewpoint. My work takes me out but I don't feel I step outside my faith. I fulfil all my Islamic obligations. In Islam the emphasis is on amal and ilm, on seeking knowledge and in consistent action. If a woman is part of society isn't it her duty to contribute towards its development and well-being?'

According to Jilani the hold of religion is more on Muslim women than men. All the rules and regulations imposed by mullahs start and end with women. Women, they say, should stay at home, wear a burqa when they go out, should not go out alone, not talk to a man in public or study in a class alongside men. A Muslim woman finds herself an easy victim. A man can utter three words and separate her with a divorce. And if she remarries no one will respect her in society. If there is a case of adultery and a man and woman are caught, it is the woman who is held responsible. Her pregnancy provides the proof and the man goes scot-free. Fifty per cent of Muslim families still do not allow women to take jobs. They are afraid that they will then lose their shame and not find the right husbands. Why do you need to work when we are here they say. That lends them honour and helps to keep their hold on women. A woman will not work if her husband has a job. She enjoys being protected as a possession. She may get educated but prefer to stay home eating, sleeping, shopping, going to the cinema. Their husbands want that. With the movement of large numbers of men to the Gulf, values have begun to change. The money that is pouring in keeps the women in comfort. They almost prefer their men away. He would have been a nuisance if he was at home. Away, he provides the money and comfort. Money has loosened the relationship of trust between man and woman, between parents and children. What the children used to learn naturally at home they now do in madrasas. Women have lost their morals, become more showy, less caring of family and relatives. The burqa has become an anachronism, worn as it is over snazzy clothes and painted faces. Their faces have changed, as has a civilization that once drew its inspiration from a deep faith.

'In a culture that is increasingly getting materialistic, specially among the poor who were deprived in the old city, man is turning out to be an instrument of easy money,' says Jilani. She quotes from one of her own stories, where she has portrayed two women fighting over the property of a husband who was killed in a communal riot. His provident fund is more important to them than his being alive. Both the wife and mother fight over it. All those aspects that suit human greed are dug out and the blame is put on religion, mourns Jilani. 'Look at the question of dahej or dowry. In Islam you are meant to fix a meher which you can afford. There was no dowry in the Prophet's time. A woman when married was given the necessities, her rights which were a one-third share. Today even Muslim girls are being burnt if they bring insufficient dowry. It is the material tenor of the time.'

Socially aware and concerned, Jilani has stepped out of the frame. Yet there is about her a quality of tentativeness, the kind women project who have taken the first step but are afraid to go further. 'I am a writer. I attend writers' meets and sit with men. Yet I am an Islamic woman,' she reiterates. 'I take care of my house, my husband, teach my children about Islam and the rituals connected with it.'

Chand Babu's Daughters

'I go out of the house but never alone'

 They are in the interiors, around a courtyard that has trees of jamun and fig. In the dalaan, a covered verandah floored by a large rug, is spread a white chandni. Three women are seated around a dastar khan, a dining cloth, over which is laid a simple lunch—a platter of rice, a dish of marag, an Arab meat curry cooked in its own juices and spiked with black pepper, and suleimani chai, plain dark tea brewed without sugar. Breaking bread with a guest is an old Arab custom that continues to be prized in Barkas, a community on the outskirts of Hyderabad, that claims an Arab ancestry. Known for their fierce loyalty and their spirit of sacrifce, the Arabs of Barkas were brought from distant Yemen and hired to guard the palaces, the treasures and the women who belonged to the Nizams of the state. Settled in what were then referred to as barracks, now distorted to Barkas, they retain their desert culture, take pride in their genealogy and sometime to speak a language, the pure Arabic of Yemen, in which they claim the Koran was revealed.

'Come home and share lunch with us,' Chand Babu had said when I encountered him in the big mosque, one of eight in Barkas.

Through a labyrinth of sun-stained streets he leads the way, past rows of white brick houses with blue doors and blue windows. We enter one such house through the baithak, the men's sitting room. Lined on a wall are photographs, all of men, revered ancestors garbed in Arab robes. Not a single woman figures in the group portraits.

I am struck by the poise of the women as they sit leisurely, taking their time to eat and thank God for each morsel. They invite me to join them as Chand Babu withdraws to do his ablutions and offer his afternoon prayers. He will not eat till he has finished his prayers. His elderly wife, whose ears are pierced with gold rings, places before me a bowl of grapes and figs from her own yard. Baaghbaani, tending the garden, is the family vocation, traditional to the Arabs of Barkas. We grow figs, the fruits of paradise and guavas that are very beneficial for health, she whispers. Her reed-like voice is kind, her manner gentle. She speaks little but her silence radiates warmth. Her elder daughter shows a readiness to talk while the younger one, dressed in a modern embroidered kaftan, chatters, unveiling her Gulf experience. 'I go out of the house but never alone. My husband always escorts me.' That's how she managed to travel from Barkas to Abu Dhabi!

'Our girls continue to be very protected,' says Chand Babu as he leads me back into the men's baithak. A woman, in his experience, has always been a creature of the home. She observes strict purdah, never walks on the street or goes to the cinema, and only visits relatives when the occasion demands it. 'Some girls have begun to go to school,' says Chand Babu in a manner that appears apologetic. 'But we take them out after a few years. We do not want them to work. Our girls are very obedient.' That was why, he explains, the Arabs would come in hordes to marry them. Also, as the oil boom enriched the Arabs, they came and married the Deccan Muslims cheap. Now, the trend has declined. Most of them had four wives and friction arose. The girls would get a divorce and return. 'They are entitled to their rights there,' Chand Babu says. 'Within six weeks the girl or her family can go to court and demand their benefits. They don't face the kind of difficulties they do here. There is no dowry among the Arabs. No girl is burnt or tortured for the lack of it. They follow the Shariat more strictly, are more conscious of Islam than we are. With money though, change is creeping in. The young have become lazy, more showy, more daring in looks and manner. The Prophet had once expressed his worry that he was not afraid of his people being poor. He was afraid that they would become too rich.'

The Nawab's Great Grand-Daughters

'I have to go out and be like other women'

'If royalty means blue blood then we don't have it,' say the three sisters. They are the great-grand-daughters of Nawab Wajid Ali Shah who live in Matia Burj in Bengal where the legendary Nawab died in exile. 'Our grandfather preferred to leave his kingdom, rather than witness the bloodshed of millions he loved and ruled. He left Lucknow and spent the rest of his life in Matia Burj outside Calcutta, turning it into another Lucknow.' Abdul Halim Sharar, the chronicler who spent part of his childhood in Matia Burj, endorses their view. 'There was the same bustle and activity, the same language, style of poetry, conversation and wit. There were the same learned and pious men, the opium addicts reciting the same tales. The observances of Muhurrum, the lamentations, and imambaras, where the tazias of the Prophet's grandsons are kept to commemorate their martyrdom were exactly as in Lucknow. In 1887 the king suddenly closed his eyes forever and it seemed as though all one had seen was a dream and all one had heard was a story.'

Matia Burj today crumbles outside Calcutta. The garden mansions that the late Nawab built by the riverside now exist as factories and railway offices. The boulevard meant for royal walks is choked with traffic and noise. Of the palaces that remain the first houses a mausoleum of the dead Nawab. The children of the neighbourhood gather in its empty verandahs to learn and recite verses from the Koran. His grandson, who carries the title of Prince, lives in a room atop a steep stone staircase. He travels to Calcutta to go to the races and visit his city home where the larger family gathers during holidays. It is an old bungalow built by his grandmother Begum Hazrat Mahal who stayed on in Awadh and continued her struggle against the British. When she lost her last battle she withdrew to the seclusion of an exile in Nepal. She remains an example of strength and courage in the family.

I have trouble locating the entrance of the mansion she raised for her descendants. The basti has crowded around and hidden it from the lane. I enter through a shop, walk up dark steps into a house with a terrace. A large divan covered with a white sheet and stacked with round bolsters awaits in the manner of a welcome. A few ladies glowing with courtesy emerge from the interiors. They are the great-granddaughters of the Nawab. They conduct me gently into a small bedroom where we sit ceremoniously on beds and settle down to talk. I struggle to hear the gentle voices that with clarity and precision compete with the street noise that floats upward.

'If you cut my veins you won't find blue blood,' says Talat Fatima, eldest of the three sisters. 'Apart from giving us a good feeling, royalty has given us little else. It was never a golden cage for us. It gave us visions of our own tradition, made us feel part of history. It was more an affirmation of our genealogy than a means of livelihood. Today it is not even a source of income. It will not take us anywhere. Our actions perhaps will. Our great-grandmother is remembered for the battles she waged and won. Our battles are small. We fight them each day our own way.' Her voice is soft and resilient, more pragmatic than aloof.

Royalty never enclosed her in a palace nor put her behind the inscrutable veil. She wore no burqa through her years in school and college. Graduating with a degree in law she married a man who allowed her to stay outside purdah and even take a job as a teacher. 'Though my mother-in-law wore purdah my husband did not insist that I should. He would not have objected even if I chose to be veiled. That's what freedom means,' she states breezily. In the manner of a lawyer she sketches out the different freedoms guaranteed to a Muslim woman. Among Hindus a woman loses her identity after marriage. She takes on the name of her husband, even his family. After his death she cannot go back to her name or to being herself. As a widow she is reduced to the status of a maid servant. A Muslim widow, on the other hand, says Talat Fatima, is as good as a single person. No one forbids her to wear coloured clothes or jewellery. She is free to remarry and start a new life. 'I have not changed my own name after marriage. My husband advised me to keep my maiden name. Befitting the Islamic tradition, I received no dowry. My in-laws did not send a list of things they wanted nor did they raise a question when I entered their home. Today I joke with my husband and tell him that if he gives me a list it will take me two years to work and provide what he wants.'

Contrary to the norm, Talat Fatima has only two children. Family planning according to her is endorsed in Islam, self-control is taught, though abortion is not permitted. It is lack of education that makes people say otherwise. Even the mullahs who preach do not know the dictums. 'I have grown in the liberal traditions of the family, before and after marriage,' says Talat Fatima. 'If the need for travel arose I travelled alone, as I once did to Lucknow. My uncle saw me off in Calcutta, my father received me at Lucknow station. But during the journey for twenty hours I was alone. None of us have known total confinement. Nor have we known total freedom.'

Salamat Fatima, her second sister, has chosen to go back to purdah: she has married a maulvi whose family prizes the tradition. 'It is of course good,' she claims sitting between her two sisters who have given it up. 'Even if you do not observe purdah but keep your shame and dignity you are following the rules laid out by Islam. The Muslim women who live trapped in burqas are backward, they know nothing about Islam,' she lashes out. 'If they had studied the religion they would understand how progressive Islam is. Those who understand Islam live broad lives, for nothing is forbidden in our faith—education, work, travel. It only expects woman to be modest, hence the veil. If we follow Islam we must follow it in the spirit in which it is meant.'

The two sisters are articulate, well-informed, conversant with their religion. They have come a long way from the life of their mother who was put in a burqa at the age of nine, was not allowed even to go to the door if a vendor arrived, was not sent to school but taught at home. She broke her own shackles when she decided to send her three daughters to school and without the burqa. The only stricture she imposed on them was that they wear no sleeveless dresses and that they cover their heads with dupattas.

She was not highly educated but she was able to understand the meaning of the strictures. Don't break another's heart. Don't gossip, live by your own strength—these were the lessons she imparted to her daughters. 'Our family has always recognized the importance of an education that goes beyond a school. We were encouraged to meet all kinds of people, to talk and exchange ideas and understand differences. Mix with others, eat with them, know their ways. Besides knowing the Koran you must know the geography and history of the land you live in, the men who rule it. That does not mean you are not good Muslims. Those who think so have hung the wrong picture of Islam in their houses.'

Manzilat Fatima, youngest of the three sisters, has broken new ground by learning typing and shorthand after acquiring an MA. If it were not for her mother she would have become an air hostess. 'But that went beyond the norms of decency,' says Manzilat, who then chose to enter the more prestigious Indian Administrative Service. 'There is no taboo to work as long as it is decent,' she says softly. Less vociferous in her defence of Islam, she has come to terms with the demands that modern life has imposed on women. Her Islam is not that of her mother. 'The serenity and gentleness of my mother has existed because she never entered the modern world,' muses Manzilat. 'We are sinners. We don't have the strength. Our lives have changed. We follow Islam as best we can. I may not say my "five-times" prayers. But I try to be honest in whatever I do. Mine is a practical Islam. Perhaps I have not imbibed my faith as naturally as my mother. I also did not experience the strains of royalty. I can't wear the gharara-sharara and behave like a Begum. I have to go out and earn, be like other women.'

Bushra

'Greed has begun to enter Muslim homes'

Taleem Gah Niswan is a college exclusively for women, located in a quiet lane in Lucknow. It was formed by the liberal Habibullah family at the beginning of the century. Poor Muslim girls who prize learning as much as purdah, are beginning to cross their thresholds to go to this college.

Bushra enters the gate garbed in a burqa. She divests herself of the black garment and blithely walks across the sun-filled courtyard. She is a girl of eighteen with vivid black eyes and a ready smile. When I invite her for a cup of tea she gently declines. Instead she invites me to her home. The outside holds no meaning for her. She has never been out in the city by herself, she tells me, except when she comes to school.

An incident recounted later by her teacher reveals her isolation. 'One evening Bushra was stranded in the bazaar with her sister. No rickshaw was available. Seeing the two girls, a lady in a car stopped and offered a ride. Tired of waiting, the girls accepted. Once in the car they were terrified. What if the lady were to drive away with them? When she stopped the car at the first red light the girls jumped out telling her that their house was across the street.' Such fears go back deep, to a childhood drilled by the vague don'ts of religion rather than the do's. Some of these are slowly being questioned by young women who have begun to go to schools.

Bushra lives in a joint family house built around a courtyard green with trees, the only open space for women. On the entrance door hangs a curtain. Around the courtyard are rooms accommodating an entire joint family. In the first one lives an old uncle who has published an Urdu weekly since the year 1938. In the next room lives a spinster aunt. Across from her, in a set of two rooms, Bushra lives with her parents. She ushers me into a small room enclosed with net curtains. It is the family parlour furnished with cane chairs, new and unused, a coffee table on which rest plates of biscuits and bananas. Through a chink in the curtains I see the other room. It is larger, has a cot in a corner on which lies an old man, her father. In another corner, placed conspicuously, is a large television set. Huddled on the floor is a group of neighbourhood children watching the Sunday morning serial. It is an episode from the *Mahabharata*, the Hindu epic that is equally popular among the Muslims, even a family as orthodox as Bushra's. 'My mother leaves the room when they sound the conch that announces its beginning. But I enjoy it,' says Bushra in a soft voice. 'We must see the good in other religions and learn from them.'

Bushra means good tidings. She was given the name before she was born in the hope that she would be a boy. Third in a row, Bushra arrived, another girl. The name though remained, tied to a family's broken hope. 'It was not Allah's will,' says Bushra's mother, sitting on a bench beside her daughter. She is a dark woman with a plain face, strong from the long years of struggle. Dressed in a printed georgette sari, her hair neatly rolled into a bun, she has the look of a woman who has braved life and has come to terms with whatever it has bestowed on her.

'No, I did not get what a woman expects from marriage,' she states without emotion. 'It was doomed the day it was solemnized. My father agreed to the proposal as they were afraid I would never get a husband. I was not pretty. I had pock marks on my face. My father was a police sub-inspector and there were six girls in the family to be married off. Any proposal was welcome. They mourned when they saw the groom. He was a sickly man who worked as a peon in a court. But it was too late. I never got a husband's love or protection. I have lived suppressing my nafs, my desires. I just bore the pain, telling no one. You fall in people's eyes when you bare yourself. When the responsibilities of the house, the children and family descended on me, I gave up purdah. One can work and remain modest. As my girls are.'

As she tells her tale, Bushra, seated beside her, silently sheds tears. 'May God never give any woman the life of my mother,' she whispers.

Her mother never went to school. In the village where she grew up there was no school, no shop, no post office. The nearest school was a mile away, and in any case girls were not allowed to go. She learnt her elementary Urdu at home so that she could read and write letters. 'I have no degree. I know no English. I could not go out and work,' she says, looking back at lost time with a long regret. 'But I did whatever work I could at home like sewing clothes, cooking for parties. I could even repair a broken wall myself. I never had enough money, though, even to buy new clothes for my girls for Eid. Wear what you have even if it is not new, I would tell them. To be frugal and live within one's means is part of our faith.'

Bushra's mother allowed her girls to go to college. They even played volleyball. But she turned down a proposal for Bushra, when the groom's family demanded a scooter as part of the dowry. 'Isn't the girl herself a gift,' she asks, quoting the instance of Fatima, the Prophet's daughter, who got in her dowry a camel skin to sleep on, a pillow filled with date palm leaves to rest her head on and a set of six wooden bowls to serve food to guests! The future that looms before her daughters, however, does not fit into the framework of such an ideal. Her girls have stepped out. Without losing their modesty they have gone to college and acquired degrees. They will perhaps get jobs that improve their chances in the marriage market. Muslim men have begun to accept girls who have jobs, I am told, they sometimes even insist that their wives work. They have got used to the money.

'I don't care if I get married or not,' says Bushra. 'But I must get a good job. If I marry a man who understands me I will not work. No, not because I believe that it is not right to work but because I would like to give my best to my home and children. As my mother did.'

Intezar means to wait. It is perhaps this waiting so ingrained in the spirit of her name that has helped steel Bushra's mother. In her own neighbourhood she knows girls who are languishing in their courtyards despite their degrees. Greed has changed the tone of life in Muslim homes, admits Intezar. The demand now is for girls who have gone to a convent school, who speak English, who bring with them a dowry that includes a television set, a video, possibly a car, if not at least a scooter. A neighbour's daughter, she broods, was set afire because she brought no dowry. The family, who live in a small bare house, are dazed not by the tragedy as much as by their own poverty. 'We're so poor we could not give a dowry and save our child,' they cry. 'Where are the men who preach Islam?' questions Intezar. 'Why don't they come and save these poor souls who have neither read the Koran nor understand its teachings. All that they know is the curse of poverty.' Yet, Intezar waits. Someday the right young man will appear who will appreciate her daughter's inner wealth.

Saleha

'Why should I pray and fast out of fear'

Well-born, well educated, Saleha is a teacher in a convent school. She wears no burqa and drives her own car, unveiled. That's as far as her liberation goes: she continues to live with her widowed mother and a spinster aunt who discreetly control her life.

The three women live in one part of a sprawling house, the rest of it is rented to offices. There are no men in the family except a male servant and his young boy whom Saleha pampers as if he was her own child. Her father is dead, her brothers have migrated to bigger cities, her sisters are married. She finds herself left behind to tend a mother, an aunt and ancestral property. 'I stay here not because of a need but because I have affection for my mother. I have never lived away from the family. If someday I feel the need to, I will.'

Bound to each other by kinship and fear, the three women lean on each other, support each other, sometimes even resent each other's presence. 'For days we do not talk to each other,' admits Saleha. 'We lie on different beds and read. My mother reads aloud romances from *Pakeezah Anchal*, an Urdu family magazine, to my aunt. They spend their mornings reading the Koran. In the evenings we watch television. When we talk, it is always family gossip.'

Unlike the two older women who have aged in a secluded home, Saleha has spread her wings. She even has a room of her own, furnished in the style of the day with ethnic embroideries, bright coloured cushions and plenty of books. The rest of the house has not changed through the years. Takhts covered with white sheets lie in verandahs, on the terrace. A takht occupies a place of eminence in a Muslim home. The lady of the house spends a great deal of time sitting on it. She prays on the takht, takes her siesta on it in the afternoons, invites her friends to join her for tea, gossip and sympathy. Saleha's mother reclines on one, reading, while her aunt prays on another. Their way of life has remained almost unchanged despite the decline of a lifestyle that is associated with the taluqdars of Lucknow, became a visible urban élite in Avadh after the disappearance of the Nawabs.

Born in a taluqdar's house, Saleha's mother had a luxurious childhood. A governess taught her English so that she could decipher the names of medicines, read telegrams and write letters. It was unique in those times to have a governess. Though she was an English woman she did not impose her religious norms on the girls. She taught them what their mother wanted. 'She would wake us up dutifully at the crack of dawn for our fajr prayers,' recalls Saleha's mother. Reticent to talk at first, she agrees to gradually unfold the drama of her life, which is reminiscent of many that continue to be enacted in traditional Muslim homes.

'My life changed after marriage,' she begins in a tone that is flat, drained of energy. 'My husband was not well off. He had four sisters to support. I had to cook, scrub dishes and do all the housework. It was not very comfortable for a few years.' To understate one's sufferings is part of her ethical code. The fact that she married a man below her status, a cousin brought up in her house, indicates the spirit of brotherhood that guided her household. 'Taking care of poor relatives is an aspect of a Muslim home,' she asserts gently. 'My .father thought that only boys in the family should marry in high circles, not girls.'

Did her husband give her the security she needed? She evades the question, then with an effort steps back into a past that looms darkly behind her. 'His elder brother's widow came to stay with us. He gave more deference to my sister-in-law than to me. Her word was an order in the house. He perhaps did not realize that he was torturing me. He did, though, in many subtle ways. He knew for instance that I hated being alone. But he would always return late at night. I would wait for him beyond midnight but was not allowed to ask why he was late. Now I feel that way again when Saleha goes out at night. I can't sleep until she returns. I keep all doors and windows locked.'

What is she afraid of ? 'The cat,' she states taking me by surprise. 'From childhood I have dreaded cats.' Saleha too is afraid of cats. Once when a cat jumped on her, she fainted. 'That fear I have inherited from my mother,' she says accusingly. What she has not inherited is the fear of God. 'Why should I pray and fast out of fear?' she exclaims. 'Am I less of a Muslim because of it?'

'Not less but you are going away from your farz, your duty. When you read the Koran you will realize how important it is,' says her mother. Saleha has read the Koran in translation. She will not recite it on someone's death as is expected in the family. 'How can the dead man get benediction if I read the Koran? Isn't the Koran more a book of conduct that tells us how to live life?' she questions. 'I have fulfilled my duty by teaching you how to read it. The rest hinges on you,' her mother reiterates. 'In my mother's eyes I negate my goodness by not reading the Koran and not performing my namaz. And I am not being good if I go out alone or socialize in circles where men are present. She panics the moment I go out of her presence.'

And yet Saleha chooses to stay in her mother's house. 'If I had a creative profession my mother would have become a barrier. Now she is just a nuisance. She makes me feel guilty when I go out and she stays up.'

She recalls how once she was to go to Calcutta to attend a friend's wedding. Her mother had agreed to let her go. They even discussed the clothes and jewels she should take. Then on the day she was to leave, she found her mother violently sick.

'I did not even comfort her. I just sat and stared. Perhaps I should cancel my trip I said. "Perhaps you should," she mumbled. When I went out to send a telegram to my friend and returned I found her moving around the house as if nothing had happened. I sat on the roof for two days and wept.'

Saleha is a single woman. She has not married for she has yet to meet a man who is ahley-kitaab, one who follows her Book of Faith. Her mother will not accept any other. 'If I ever marry it will be a simple ceremony. I want to be able to go out and tell my friends that I got married yesterday.' Until then it will be she and her mother.

Nayab Jehan and Shah Jehan

'Is it not a man's faith to care for a woman?'

In the village of Khushal Ganj, Nayab Jehan grew up pampered, the only girl of six children. Now married, her great sadness is that she has borne five daughters and no son. 'My mother was luckier than me,' she says. 'The girls will grow up and go away to their husband's homes. A son would have been my support. A girl can never give that support, even if we send her to school.' She tells the story of a girl in the village who had been sent to school and who had later become a teacher. 'When she goes out the whole village stares at her. Look how she walks. She has lost all shame,' they say.

We are seated in her open courtyard that she considers more respectable than her mother's. For not even a boy of fifteen is allowed in its circle. No women strangers can come in as they do in her mother's house. Such strict purdah is a sign of status in a village like Khushal Ganj. Since her marriage, Nayab Jehan has not stepped out of her courtyard, not even to go to her mother's home. She is not allowed to stand in her doorway which overlooks a wide empty square.

'That makes no difference,' says Nayab Jehan in a tone that is self-righteous. 'Once when Bibi Fatima, daughter of the Prophet, went to the door at the call of a blind man, her father admonished her. He is a blind man, said Bibi. But you are not, answered the Prophet.'

Nayab Jehan recounts the episode to justify her own seclusion.

As a young girl she roamed free in the village. During the rains she would put up swings of rope and sing like a lark. 'Today I dread to go out alone. I don't have the courage. I feel weak.'

When she married and came to her new home the restrictions imposed on her by her mother-in-law and her husband irked her. Every girl after marriage is supposed to stay home, she consoled herself. As one day merged with the next, she began to lose the lilt in her limbs. And she began to see her seclusion as a blessing.

A sad-looking young woman, Nayab Jehan lacks the open looks of her mother, who remains agile despite her fifty-odd years. What the mother has learnt from life, Nayab Jehan has failed to gather from the hundreds of books she claims she has read. 'My mother worked all her life. I stay home and am provided for.' She has gained respectability in her own eyes but lost her freedom.

The name Khushal Ganj means 'prosperity' but the paths that lead to this village of a hundred Muslim homes are choked with mud and stagnant water.

'Even if it is dukh-hal, a time filled with suffering, it is His giving.'

The man who makes this statement is a farmer like most of the others in the village. He is a patriarch by birth and by tradition. His fields bloom when Allah wills. But the women in the village backyards never do. For that too, he believes silently, is the will of Allah.

The men of Khushal Ganj are out in the open, beside fields of hay, under sheds without walls. Their women are crouched on charpoys in inner courtyards where the family cattle, stray dogs and cats also live. Many of them sit bent over yards of white muslin. They are weaving delicate designs in thread, traditionally known as chikan work, a craft that dates back to royal times, passed on from mother to daughter. The voice of the muezzin from the village mosque trails into their airless spaces proclaiming the oneness of God. But does not God's Will proclaim also the oneness of things, and isn't woman part of that open world? Questions such as these are not raised in Khushal Ganj. If a woman raises her voice and is heard she faces the danger of losing her hijab, her veil. That spells doom not only for herself but for the home. In the preservation of her shame lies her man's honour.

'Is it not a man's deen to care for his women,' asks Shah Jehan, mother of Nayab Jehan. 'Now that I am an old woman, I have learnt to speak. When I had strength in my limbs I was treated worse than a bull.' Her husband ate, drank and slept on his cot while his fields lay fallow. At sixty-four, he continues to do the same.

'If he asked for a glass of water and I tarried a while his rod descended on me. I had failed in my duty, he would scold. It never occurred to him that he too had failed in his.

'Like all men, he only understands the dung of cows. Whether a woman has oil in her hair and a bangle in her hand is not his concern. No woman dares ask a man for a few coins to fulfil her desires. Will not Allah ask him if it is not his duty to provide for his wife? Is his task only to wield a stick if the bread is not hot and the curry is without spice? When a man's strength is not shared, when a woman stands alone how can she preserve a noor and bring radiance to the house? If I was a servant in a rich man's house I would have eaten apples and got roses in my cheeks. All I got here was a bit of milk from the family cow.'

'All I had was my own strength and that of Allah,' she claims. 'There was the farm but no one to work on it. And there was no money. I begged from door to door. At times I wanted to jump in the village well and end my life. Then I thought of the children God had blessed me with. That was my khuli daulat, an open treasure that nobody could take away from me.'

Revere the womb that brought you into the world, says the Holy Koran. Shah Jehan's children respect their mother, understand her struggle and the strength of her convictions. It was her eldest son, who works in a government office, who bought for her from his first pay a new set of clothes that she dare not wear. For she has worn only old and discarded clothes. 'All I know is the salwar that my mother stitched with thirty odd patches.'

The first time she wore sandals was on her wedding day. They came with the bridal set that consisted of a red suit, green bangles, a string of black beads and a large nose ring. The joy of being a bride lasted a day. The nose ring that circled half her face was taken away the next day—it had been rented for the occasion.

Shah Jehan shed her bridal finery and got into old clothes to work in her husband's field. Her day began at the crack of dawn when the milkman came to take away the buffalo and ended late at night when he returned. They were long days filled with work— weeding the field, grinding the wheat, feeding the buffalo, sweeping the home and the yard, cooking, cleaning, caring for six children.

'I came into this house not to be its glory but to be its servant.' She smiles at the irony veiled in her name. She was not meant to be lord of the universe as the name suggests.

'Mine has been a life of suffering,' she says, in a tone that is matter of fact. 'The girls today can't take the struggles I faced. They will pull the braid of the mother-in-law and the beard of the father-in-law if they don't get their terrycot suits, their powder and lipstick.'

Her daughter, she says, has dozens of clothes, some imported from Pakistan. Her husband buys things for her—bangles, powder, oil and lipstick. He has lent her dignity by putting a veil on her face.

'If I am happy it does not mean I should always be happy,' mutters Nayab Jehan. 'If there is no salt in the house I have learnt to cook the bread without it for I can't go out and buy it. In my mother's time if there was no flour for the bread she would grind the wheat herself. She had the strength to do it. Her husband never cared. Mine does. When we were first married he would take me to the cinema and go visiting relatives. Now he can't as he is gone with the jamaat. He travels to villages and teaches the peasants to walk on the road of deen—to pray, to fast, to be good Muslims. I take pride in his mission. He has given me children, a house and respectability. Whether I am happy in this life or not is irrelevant. I should find happiness in the next life. This life is only a preparation for that sukoon, the peace in after life.'

Popli in the Desert

'Islam is a matter of instinct'

The road to Popli's house is not marked. She lives in the wilds of Banni, a desert that sprawls across the Rann of Kutch in Western India. Her forefathers traversed its salt-flecked white wastes on moonlit nights, covered in white sheets to escape attention. Five hundred years ago it was a hijra that led them from Arabia to Sindh and then to Kutch where a benign Raja gave them shelter. They settled in the wilderness guarding his borders and their own lives and truths, imbibed from a Bedouin faith that they had left far behind. With a heaven above and the earth below, the faith of a distant desert, simple, often impalpable, survived. For those who live in the desert where there are no shut spaces religion is a matter of instinct, as are man's relations to man. And that is the way of Islam in Banni where Popli lives.

I travel long hours through barren wastes to reach the house of Gul Beg, Popli's father, chieftain of the tribe, famed for his cattle and his hospitality. My eyes itch at the monotony of the landscape—miles of bleakness where nothing grows except the babul tree, the colour of ash. Lizards bore holes in the sands and disappear, the only sign of life. There is no other sound, no other life for endless miles. And then suddenly like a vision I see ahead what seems an oasis—a cluster of finely thatched conical roofs, the bhungas of Dhordo, the homes of the Mutuwa tribes, the cattle-breeders of Banni.

The welcome is simple but traditional. A man dressed in a

coloured lungi awaits me. Gul Beg looks like an Arab. He leads me into the main bhunga, a home that he has raised with his own hands. The circular hut's white walls glint with chipped mirrors. From the roof hang traditional bhurat embroideries crafted by mothers and grandmothers, their skills learnt in the desert of Sindh. Cushions covered in brilliant mashroo silk lie on naked rope charpoys, their rich colours filling the empty space. There are no other furnishings except for a ceiling fan that hangs from the conical roof. A gift from a friend in Yemen, it is strangely alien. Sitting on the mud floor I feel a cool breeze and the desert seems far away.

'Little in our lives has changed,' says Gul Beg, sitting crosslegged on the ground. 'When our ancestors came to Banni it was a total wilderness. There were no roads, no train, no radio, no hospital or school. We roamed free like our animals. Nothing grew except grasses, good for cattle. We became maldaris, cattle-breeders. Food was cheap and health better. Our men were tall and well-built, their minds were free. When a man died at eighty we said he died young.'

Like the men were the women, sturdy in body and in spirit. They walked to collect wood and gobar, fetch water. They would grind their own flour on a chakki, cook food in clay vessels on wood, not gas stoves. They were in charge of the household, sharing their tasks with the men, enjoying an equality not seen outside the desert. 'And yet none of our women have gone beyond two kilometers. They do not wear purdah but jealously guard their honour. *Hum dil ka purdah kartey hain sirif aankh ka nahin'*—we veil not just our eyes but our hearts, our feelings.

As Gul Beg traces his family tree I see neat ties of kinship emerge and somewhere in the hoary past an eponymous ancestor. Three Bapu Mians and two Gul Begs are inscribed on the chart and he, the third Gul Beg, heads a clan of 150, all claiming descent from one father. 'We marry within our kutumb, our community. No, it does not weaken the breed. It is allowed by Shariat. It keeps us happy and united,' he explains.

In Dhordo the entire clan is bound by marriage and kinship ties, sharing joys and sorrows, clinging to norms and rituals that are unspoken but rigid. In such a community friendships matter. If a man dies no food is cooked in his house for four days. It is cooked and sent by relatives. And if there is a marriage, all expenses are shared. Mehmaan-nawazi is a revered tradition and no seeker who comes to the door goes away empty-handed.

'To serve the world is the only purpose of life, it is our akhlaq, part of our Islamic upbringing,' says Gul Beg, summing up the philosophy of a desert people. He recounts the story of an evil woman who once gave water to a god. Years later when her grave was dug they found no bones but a shining light. 'God is Rahim and Karim, the Compassionate and the Generous One. He holds the strings of our lives. Nothing rests in our hands. We come empty-handed and go away empty-handed.'

When there are no shut spaces, when people live on a wide empty earth with a heaven above and the stars so close, God too is very near. There is a homeliness about the Arab God. He pervades the dailyness of life, the food that is eaten, the guest who arrives. Inshallah is the most familiar of the words in a desert. 'We all know what religion is, what is gunah, what is savaab, evil and good. Even a child knows,' says Gul Beg. And what they know is not learnt nor transmitted by the teachings of mullahs. It is a matter of instinct.

A serenity reigns over Gul Beg's township. Like Biblical princesses the women adorn their ears with large gold rings, cover their arms with ivory bangles. They wear garments that they have embroidered in silk and bedecked with glinting mirrors, a craft they have learnt from their mothers. Popli is among them. Garbed in brilliance, she enters with a jug of water to wash the visitor's hands and feet. She is followed by an older woman who carries food—a platter of goat meat and rice cooked in the desert tradition. 'She is my wife,' says Gul Beg indulgently as the older woman smiles faintly and withdraws. 'No woman in Banni is as good as her,' he continues. 'She is up before the cock crows to do her morning namaz. She fasts all the thirty days of Ramzan. She works hard, stays healthy, looks after the family, the goats and the guest.'

His concept of an ideal woman hinges on simple principles that are not his own but those that have been passed down. A woman should be loyal to her husband, be frugal in home expenses, preserve her dignity and remain rooted to the home and the family. Popli continues the tradition, a child of the desert following in her mother's footsteps.

She takes pride in the things she has learnt from her mother. 'Watching her I have learnt to pray, to cook, to look after the guest. She is not an educated woman but she is a good soul. I am not as good as her. I don't have her sabr and her capacity to bear suffering. I cannot adhere as strictly to the times of prayer as I have my children. But my faith is as staunch as hers. I read the Koran and religious books and draw strength from them.'

Though Popli never went to school, as there was none in the village, she learnt to read the Koran from a relative who was a Hafiz, a Koranic scholar. She can also read Urdu and Sindhi and has picked up some English from visitors. But like the other women in the clan, she has never been outside Banni. She has not seen the cinema but has begun to listen to the radio. A day in her life is not very different from her mother's. She awakes with the azaan, prays, cleans the house, cooks, makes buttermilk. Her children go to the school that started in a neighbouring village a year ago. She plans to withdraw them though when they reach the age of ten for she considers Islami talim more important than an education that readies people only for jobs. 'Ours is not a city culture,' she says. 'What we need here is what we learn from our mothers.'

Girls, even in the desert, continue to be considered parayi, belonging to another. They go away after marriage. Hence they get the regard but not an equal share in the family property. They get only one-eighth, are allowed to take away the quilts they make, may be a goat or a cow. Sons though get a share of the animals and money. Popli who married her uncle's son did not leave the village. She stays with her husband in a nearby bhunga sharing the kitchen with her mother.

Popli receives me in her home along with her husband, a soft-spoken, reticent man. A spirit of equality binds the two. Friends since childhood, they quietly guard the mutual regard they have for each other. 'Before marriage I never prayed,' says her husband. 'Watching Popli, sitting with her and listening to her I have learnt. She is more educated than I am. She can read Arabic, Urdu and Sindhi. She is my teacher.' Like Gul Beg, Popli's husband owns cattle and has a flour mill. He used to drive trucks on the high roads but after marriage gave it up to help Popli with bhurat, her embroidery business. He goes on a horse to the surrounding villages to give and collect the work that women do in their homes. Popli has begun to organize their sale through visitors who come to Banni. 'Our women do not go out and work,' he explains. 'Popli does handicrafts and as she cannot go around, I do it for her. She does not say that business is only a man's job nor do I ever tell her that housework is a woman's job. We share our work and our life. Popli has got everything good in her.'

'However good a woman is, it is man who is badshah,' rejoins Popli. 'He is her Taj.' What if her husband takes another wife as permitted in Islam? 'The question does not arise,' answers Popli. 'We have love between us and children. No, a man does not have lust when he is happy.'

'If I marry again I cannot provide a home to another wife. I am a man of small means. And I don't have the strength. I am aware of my responsibilities,' adds her husband. 'My brother has been married for thirty years and has no children. Despite his wife telling him to take another wife he has not remarried. In the city men are more that way. In Banni we are isolated from those corrupting influences and we are together. Our community will not accept a girl from outside. If an outsider comes the bond is weakened. If they come from good stock the marriage is good. If the wall is strong then the picture that hangs on it is good. We live within the perimeters of the clan. What the clan thinks subconsciously becomes our thought. As we never leave the kutumb we have not begun to think differently.'

Despite a school that has been started and the arrival of radio Banni remains isolated from much of the outside world. As do its women. They do what has always been done, their mode of food and dress, even their speech, has not varied despite a growing contact with visitors. In the seeming monotony of that life a serenity prevails.

'What is this life? It is the other life that matters,' says Popli, still in her twenties and vibrant. 'In this life the more the suffering, the better it is for an after life. The Prophet had said that if we deny ourselves the comforts of a good life here we are promised a better life in the Hereafter. He never let his daughter wear a necklace of gold. This world, he said, was not important, it is only a preparation for the other world.'

Namaz is an ikhrar, an understanding with God. It means I bow before you. You accept me as I stand before you, forgive my sins. A lot of strength comes with prayer. God accepts if we pray in good faith, she says. 'For He is always watching us. I don't have that much intelligence to know what God is like. But I know He exists. Otherwise how are we all made? Who put us in the mother's womb, gave us a face, a temperament; made some fair, some dark, each different from the other? I think a lot about these things, and about God.'

Shumsunissa

'Allah in the river and field'

 The year of her birth was a year of famine. The pot of paddy her mother had hidden in the earth the year before had turned sour and had begun to smell. There was not enough rice gruel to feed the child. The year that followed had ravaged the fields with floods. That was followed by another year of famine. Her blind mother counts year after year of disasters till her memory fails and her withered face melts into a remote smile. In her name is wrapped the radiance of the sun. When she was born in a village not far from Calcutta the mullah had opened the Koran seeking God's help. From the pages of the Holy Book had sprung the word 'Shums' which in Arabic means the sun. And so Shumsunissa was named. Born of a mother who was blind to the sun's light, and a father who went away quietly one morning and never returned.

In the in-between years that never changed colour, Shums grew within the hedges of the paddy fields. She learnt to plant and weed the tender green and when the season turned she went with her mother from house to house to husk paddy for a measure of grain. When the village ponds were full in the rains she helped gather small fish in a basket and hawked them in the bazar. Nature surrounded and sustained her, even whilst it raged in famines and in floods. At fifteen she found herself married to Badal Mian, reconciling herself to a life with a man who was slightly deranged. Till one day he too disappeared and never returned, leaving a little boy as his memory.

Shumsunissa earns to feed him and her mother. She has no land of her own—she works on others' fields and is paid in kind. She brings home a sack of rice and sometimes dried fish. In the evenings she embroiders fans and sells them in the weekly bazar. When sales are good, she buys pumpkin or spinach for a curry and a biscuit or candy for her little boy. In the last year she has bought nothing else for the house. When she sold twelve fans to a lady from the city she bought a sari for her mother.

She herself owns only one Tangail sari. When it is torn another will come. From where? Allah will arrange it, she says. Shumṣunissa has no dreams for herself. Someday, maybe a piece of land where she will grow her own paddy and continue to live an honest life. 'Inshallah,' she murmurs. She does not pray to Allah. But as the seasons change, the fields ripen and the rivers run, she makes offerings to those spirits that she deems godly. She joins the village women in their offerings to Lokhi, the Goddess who guards the paddy fields. Hindu women in her village fashion her in the image of Lakshmi while Muslim women revere her as a ferishta, the angel who brings fertility and plenty to the land. Much in the same way they pacify Khizr Pir, the spirit who guards the rivers. Khizr who belongs to the Muslim mythology of Bengal has interfused with the Aryan Hindu myths. Together they make a landscape of religious ritual and tradition that are revered equally by Muslims and Hindus.

Shumsunissa's Allah does not reside in a mosque. She sees Him everywhere. She bends silently to his fury when the floods wash away her fragile shelters. She bows to Him in gratitude when the paddy turns green and there is plenty of rice for the three in her family. 'Our lives,' she says 'depend on Him. He creates and He destroys. We only live like ants.'

Mumtaz

'Islam is not a force in my life. Humanism is'

 'My grandmother would wake us up early in the
mornings when she heard the call of azaan. She
would not tell us to pray but to sing.' Born a
Muslim, Mumtaz learnt to sing like many Hindu
girls in Bengal where music commands the
sanctity of prayers. While her grandmother recited
the Koran in one room the children's voices
matched hers as they practised the musical
alphabet. It was a music teacher not a maulvi who
groomed their early years. Like all children in the
neighbourhood Mumtaz went to school and
studied alongside boys. Purdah did not exist in
the village and no young woman wore a veil.
During vacations, in her grandmother's house, on the edge of a
green pond, she learnt to paint and take part in the jatras, folk
plays that were as much a part of their village as any other in
Bengal. The soil of her landscapes had been nurtured by a
century of bhakti and popular religion, resulting in the tradition
that all shared whatever their religion.

Living side by side, sharing a country the Hindus and the
Muslims of Bengal had learnt to recognize and respect each
other's differences. A mid-nineteenth century report describes
the feelings of camaraderie that prevailed in Bengal a hundred
years ago.... 'Men and women sitting in groups under trees, on
the banks of lakes, playing on the Gopi Yantra, singing and
clapping to the shouts of the name of their founder Aulchand. In
another corner a Muslim fakir, waving a brush fan, narrating in

song the history of his sect to an enraptured crowd.' The Sufis roamed the countryside much like the Bauls did. Often the songs of one religious group were indistinguishable from the other. Mumtaz remembers one old Baul singer who would wander past their house every other month singing a song of Lallan Shah, a nineteenth-century folk poet. She did not know then how radical the song was.

> If you have to make out a Muslim man (from circumcision)
> How are you to identify a Muslim woman?
> If a Brahmin man is to be recognized
> By his sacred thread
> How are you to identify a Brahmin woman?

The Bauls and the Sufis sang for all people irrespective of caste or creed, in words that made a mockery of dogma and ritual. They mingled with the more formal strains and sang in the prayer halls of Calcutta. New credos were taking birth in the big city.

When Mumtaz moved to Calcutta with her parents she found the air charged. Slogans in the city were palpable. They touched and transformed the lives of people. The spirit of the reform movements that had stirred Bengal a century ago was not dead. It had new names and new forms. Her father, a Communist, introduced her to the ideals of Marx and Mao. To his progressive friends ideologies mattered more than gods. At the new school run by the Brahmo Samaj, she was introduced to the ideas of Raja Rammohun Roy whose message was that all religion was one. And as every religion had the same end, namely the moral regeneration of mankind, each, believed Roy, needed to be reinterpreted and reassessed in a changing time. Roy, who had studied the Scriptures in Sanskrit and the Koran in Arabic, wrote in both languages espousing the universality of all moral teachings. He condemned ritual and dogma, renounced idolatry and priestcraft. Known for his advocacy of women's causes he fiercely called for the abolition of sati.

Continuing his tradition, the schools run by the Brahmo Samaj provided an English education and exposed the young to western thought and ideas which alone Roy had felt would free young minds from blind faith and superstition. Among Mumtaz's friends at school were girls whose families had stepped out of Hindu orthodoxy to embrace the ideals of Roy's Brahmo Samaj (Society of God.) In such a milieu, charged with an intense spiritual and cultural consciousness, Mumtaz became a young woman.

Later at the medical school she was one of the few Muslim women to qualify as a gynaecologist. At college she fell in love with a Hindu boy but did not marry him. Her husband was to be a Muslim with whom she not only shared a language and culture but also a faith. He transported her back into a joint family house behind whose walls a strict faith prevailed. Her father-in-law was a zealous patriarch who commanded the rhythms of the house, where everyone prayed at appointed hours and lived quiet and seemingly blissful lives in allotted spaces.

Mumtaz shared hers with three other sisters-in-law, all deeply religious women. They accepted her liberal views, and said nothing about her Marxist political background. She in turn adapted to them, even began praying to please them. 'Islam is not a force in my life,' admits Mumtaz. 'Humanism is. As I learnt from my father and from the songs of my childhood. I do not feel constrained physically or psychologically though I have come back to live in a joint family. When I do, I visit my father's house.' Mumtaz drives her own car, works long hours in the hospital and returns to share her space with a large family where life goes on oblivious of the pace of the city.

Little has changed in the neighbourhood where her father-in-law's house stands. Like everything in Calcutta. Nothing changes in the city that does not conform to the mythic patterns of its denizens. More so in Coollotola, a Muslim ghetto where Mumtaz lives. It is a constricted world of commerce and community where money is as central for survival as God. In the narrow lanes lie piles of animal skins, for the main business of the area is leather.

Mumtaz's house stands in a congested lane. We enter a small courtyard layered with cobblestones, around which are rooms where silence reigns despite the people who live in them. Everything in the house seems as it always has been, old furniture, musty drapes, masses of unused utensils. In the several rooms up and down the stairs live four units of the family. They have separate bedrooms but share one kitchen. Where meals are shared unity prevails, they say. I am served an elaborate lunch with three kinds of Bengali fish under the watchful gaze of three sisters-in-law. They smile and stare and say nothing. After the meal, where food dominates more than camaraderie, the eldest sister-in-law, a widow, ushers me into her bedroom. We settle down on the large bed and eat paan as a preparatory exercise. Mumtaz sits quietly while the elder lady plunges into a monologue, laced with drama and tears.

'I was married on 18 November, 1956 and I became a widow in March 1972,' she begins as tears fill her large, tired eyes. 'I was carrying a nine-month-old baby when my husband died. I don't know how the years have passed since his death. Just bringing up my children. My son, a doctor, is settled in the UK. A daughter is in college and will soon be married. My duty will then finish. If God then takes me up to Him I will be happy. I have nothing more to live for. I have given all that I had to my children. I never ate well nor dressed in fancy clothes, never went to a hotel or a cinema, never relaxed talking to friends on the phone or asked them over. I lived alone, cried alone.'

Should she not remarry and find a new life for herself as is permissible in Islam?

'When I was young the need for a man was not much. Now that I am old I need a swami, a companion who will share my thoughts, my life,' she wails. 'I am not literate. I can't go out and get a job. If a woman like me becomes a widow I would advise her to get remarried. But I don't have the courage to do it myself. My husband was a good man, he gave me a house, car, wealth, love, children. How can I forget all that?' she weeps. The crows in the courtyard raise a cacophony as if in sympathy.

Manubehn

'The worst is now possible. Donkeys will neigh and women will sit on chairs'

 Manubehn does not belong anymore to the village in which she was born. For she has chosen to live without a protector. The older of two daughters, married and abandoned by a husband who later married her own sister, she doggedly pursued a career. She became a village health worker, fought to have her only daughter admitted to an English medium school, continued to work on her farm near the river and walked through the village with her medical kit even whilst the men stared and the women gossiped. They did not admire her.

Courage of this sort in a woman is a questionable commodity. A woman should only have the courage to suffer but never to express her own energy. 'We like our girls married,' says one village elder, 'otherwise they will end up like Manubehn.' Does he not admire her courage to stand alone? No, he says bluntly. 'To work for a living outside one's home is the last resort of a woman who has no place in her community. It takes away her purity.'

Manubehn, a dark woman with a grave face, offers no defence. 'I would not have been able to work if the sarpanch had not given me his full support,' she mumbles when questioned. 'They scandalized even his support.'

What about her mother? Has she accepted her? Does she live with her? 'Yes,' says Manubehn. Then, she corrects herself. 'No, I live with her,' she says with a small smile. And yet she is the one who earns and runs the house.

She harbours no resentment against her mother who pushed her, and later her sister, into marriage with the same man. 'My mother thought that my sister could be happy with him,' she says flatly. Was she? 'No,' she says. He drove her out too. But the mother did not wait long. She married her off to another jahil, a boor like the first one. Will she meet the same fate also at his hands? No one holds the mother guilty. What could a poor old woman do? She wanted the best security for her girls, they say, nodding their grey heads in unison.

The mother's draped head is bowed. When she slowly raises it to the level of the circle, seated as if in judgement, I see no fear in her eyes. No bitterness or supplication. Just a veil of not knowing. 'It is she who married her two daughters in succession to one man,' says the young sarpanch of Hadgud, a village of 500 houses in Gujarat where in every other home, each man has more than two wives, if not more.

Is she guilty—this small, shrivelled, desolate woman? Tired at fifty, she bore her husband five girls and after his death lived a tenuous life with just one mission—to see her daughters settled. To settle a girl in these parts as elsewhere means finding for her a house she can call her own and a man who will play protector, even if he is not quite her own but is shared. By taking her as a wife, even if she is one of several, he puts a price on her nameless head. Ownership, however dubious or diffused, lends a woman respectability. She belongs.

On a warm June morning I have come to Hadgud to meet with Manubehn. She has brought credit to the village, I tell them. They are not convinced. Disbelief is the colour of their old eyes. 'How can a single woman change the thinking of a village buried in fear and superstitions?' says the young sarpanch as if he has read my question. 'The village is much better than it was before. Some years ago a woman could not even walk into this office. Now she comes in and sits on a chair.'

Sitting on a chair in Hadgud is a woman's ultimate defiance. 'We are heading for bad days,' mourns a village elder. 'Men seek divorce at the drop of a hat. In my days a man even without seeing a woman would get married and honour his pledge. He would treat her kindly even after taking a second wife. Now it is talaq,

- 94 -

talaq, talaq. Very easy.'

'All that is taught to a young man in Hadgud is how to mount a donkey and how to whitewash,' rejoins the sarpanch. To mount a donkey in Hadgud means to marry a girl whom he has neither known nor seen. Marriage to him is as unpredictable as riding a donkey.

Before he turns into a man he is taught his vocation—to whitewash walls. His kismet is secure as he learns to mount a donkey, ride it and stay on top of it. When the donkey begins to neigh he will have a difficult time. 'That day is not far,' quips the elder. 'The worst is now possible. Donkeys will neigh and women will sit on chairs.'

Fatima Rehman

'My religion is Islam but my culture is Malayali'

We are driving to Fatima Rehman's ancestral home. She is a retired judge, a social worker and a proud grandmother. 'My uncle was a Haji and very wise man,' she says as we drive up Highway 17 that links miles of green into a distinct landscape. 'He built schools in the twenties when few dared to send their children out of the house. When he called·out to the Muslims to learn English they threw rotten eggs at him and his workers. Studying English then meant becoming an unbeliever. He set up a society called Aikyun where girls and boys of all faiths sat together and read.' That school still remains in her native village, a cluster of small structures with red-tiled roofs. Amidst them rises a brick building that is the new school. It is crowded with children who not only learn the English that was once banned but three other languages – Hindi, their own local Malayalam, and Arabic, the language of the Holy Koran. In her mother's time women were not allowed to pray in mosques, and only a few could read the Koran. For Arabic was a language they revered but did not understand.

Today, they read the Holy Book in their own Malayalam. The khutba in the mosque is pronounced in the local language. But in Cheraman Malik mosque, said to be the oldest in India, built in A.D. 629, it is read in Arabic, the language in which, says the muezzin of the mosque, God spoke. But when a child cries, he adds, he does so in Malayalam. And when men pray to their respective gods they do so in Malayalam. Unlike imams in North India, the one who presides over the ancient mosque is dressed in a white lungi with a cloth wrapped around his chest. Resting on a grass mat he chats. What makes a Malayali a Malayali is not the language alone but also his dress, food and daily habits.

All along the road we encounter trucks and buses that carry names from St. Gregorius and Jessica to Shakila, Hasina, Ayyappa and Shanker, signs of the generations of inter-religious living that Kerala has known. We pass churches, mosques and temples assertive amidst the luxuriant green. Conspicuous too is the presence of women, standing at bus stops, in bazaars, driving up in jeeps, pulling water out of wells, wading through streams, legs exposed, carrying loads on their heads. Most of them are rural women who work in the fields and move around freely. Among them are Muslim women dressed like Hindu girls in lungi and blouse. No veils cover their bosoms, though their heads are covered with square scarves called Makana. A draped head on the Malabar coast does not signify the reticence and delicacy often associated with burqa-clad women in other parts of India.

'In Sura Noor it says you drop your eyes when you encounter a man,' says Fatima who has read the Koran in translation and understands its meanings. 'It does not say you should wrap up your body and not see men at all. When we go to Haj we see men all around. I have never worn the burqa but have always covered my head. Everyone stared at me and my sister when we wore Makanas on our heads even when we were little girls. We were the only two Muslims in school and stood out because of the head scarves. My uncle did not want Muslims to feel that sending girls to school meant not wearing the scarf and giving up modesty, an ideal enshrined in Islam. After all he was building institutions and had to set an example.'

At sixty-five, Fatima continues to do the same. She drapes her head with her pallu, the end portion of her pale silk sari. Revealing her face at this age no longer holds the danger of attracting men. But her purdah, which means draping the body and head, is symbolic of modesty and propriety. For she too must set an example like her uncle, being a pioneer in the setting up of institutions for women and children. As Founder President of the Muslim Women's Association she had helped build a school, an orphanage where 300 children are fed and clothed, taught to read, write, sew, sing and dance; an industrial unit consisting of a press and a tailoring section for women. 'These institutions are like my children,' she smiles. 'They give me the same joy. The work I do for them is for my future life after death, it will help me go to Heaven.'

As important to her life is the large extended family, her own and her husband's. We visit some of them on the way; a brother who has raised a mansion by a river in Alwaye; the ancient house of her son-in-law's mother, a structure with dark wooden beams and deep interiors where an old woman lives guarding an ancestral property; several houses of brothers shaded by old palm trees and finally her own father's house set amidst acres of coconut plantations with separate bathing tanks for men and women, a pavilion that served as the men's baithak, another where all children were born (there were no doctors or hospitals at the time), and a prayer hall.

A young woman with deep sad eyes receives us at the house. She is the widow of Fatima's brother who died a young man. She is in mourning. Silently we sit in the verandah shaded by bougainvillaeas and drink tender green coconut water from the family gardens. In the courtyard lie stretches of areca nuts and peppers drying in the sun. The young widow looks after the plantation and lives in the large house, under the discreet gaze of the ancestors whose solemn portraits hang on the walls. Fatima's brother, who is married to the widow's sister, also lives in the house and watches over her. Will she remarry? 'It is very complicated,' sighs Fatima, 'because of the children and the property. If she remarries, she will have to leave the house and go away. She is comfortable here. She has the house, the plantation, the children.'

Education has changed the marriage patterns, explains Fatima. Fewer men take more than one wife these days. Younger women no longer have more than two or three children. The Koran does not forbid family planning before conception. It even encourages coitus interruptus – self-control by men, if permitted by women. Fatima was one of thirteen children. She has a son and a daughter while her daughter only has a son. When she traces the family tree I confuse the connections, the inter-relationships. Forty-five in the family are doctors, education being an important concern from the uncle's days.

In her own childhood when she should have been playing hopscotch on the sands, as many children still do on the beaches of her native village, she was sent off with her sister to live in a small house built in town by her father so that they could go to a nearby high school. Two girls living away from the family was unheard of in Cranganore.

'But we had our nannies with us and they were like family,' says Fatima. Her father unlike her uncle was not an educated man. He could read and write enough to look after his property. But he wanted all his children to study, including the girls, and drove on his motor-bike from the plantation every day to check on them.

Her mother never did. She remained in the village, in the family house, busy in her large kitchen cooking food on stoves of firewood, crying from the smoke in her eyes. She must have been, I tell myself, like the women I had seen in the large matrilineal houses of Calicut in which the men and not the women come to live after marriage. In one large bare house with nothing but small bedrooms for couples and several kitchens buzzing with activity, I had met nearly a hundred women—mothers, sisters, daughters cooking, cleaning rice, chatting. The older ones had ears pierced with circles of gold rings sticking out like wings on fire. But these ornate wings were clipped. The women lived enclosed within walls, working days in the kitchen, waiting nights in tiny bedrooms for their husbands to visit them. Nights of passion perhaps were many but days of love few and far between.

'They are breeding places,' one man had commented. He was a Koya, a Moplah, who had migrated to the Gulf. 'My life is different,' he had said. 'My wife goes out shopping, reads magazines. My daughter has completed her M.Com. and started her own business. Our house is different. We have books. We hear music. Watch films together.'

'My parents lived separate lives,' says Fatima, bringing me back to her time. 'There was little communication or friendship between couples in the old days. Men dominated the house, controlled the purse strings. Women took care of the kitchen and the children. Today they consult and cooperate. The women work but it is more difficult as they have fewer servants. It will become worse when servants disappear and we have no one to entrust our children to. I was lucky. I could do both, have a family and work. I had old servants and my husband helped in my office work as he too was an advocate. I was a government magistrate when I started my career. I would leave my little son in the nursery and go to work. My children were never neglected. I refused a promotion for I did not want to move away from the family. If I had, I would have retired as a judge of the High Court.'

The happiest day in her life was not the day she got her law degree nor the day of her marriage when there was a big feast that the whole village was invited to share. Nor again was it when her father had died and she received her share of property, half of what her brothers got—fifteen acres of land, fifty gold sovereigns, a house and a car. 'It was when my son got his doctor's degree that I was happiest.'

Fatima has no regrets. She deems herself blessed for she has a good husband, two brilliant children and many more whom she has groomed in the institutions she has helped establish. 'I take the car in the morning and go for a round of my institutions. I come back in time for my husband to take the car to court. In the evening he goes to the club, I stay back and wait for my grand-children.'

I visit her institutions, meet the girls she has groomed who gather in a large hall and perform a welcome ceremony. They chant verses from the Koran in Malayalam and then clapping their hands, dance the Oppana, a native bridal number. Their religion is Islam but their culture is Malayali.

'The roots of this co-existence can be traced to all those nameless men who sailed the seas, settled and built bridges,' hums Fatima.

Even the name of Kerala is blessed. The story goes that the first Arabs, on their routes of discovery, were lost in the monsoon storms for endless days. They could see nothing except the fury of rains and a stormy sea. When suddenly they sighted in the distance a green horizon they raised their hands in thanksgiving and exclaimed 'Khair-Allah.' That land came to be known as Kerala.

Akbari

'Life with love moves on'

A husband died. Then, five children, all that remained of her world. The empty house tightened around her like a noose. The walls stared, more sinister than they had seemed in all those years when she lived enclosed within them. She left the house, gave up the gold and silver, the treasure that every woman so painstakingly gathers and guards through a lifetime. To give away jewels that so often epitomize for women not only security but a whimsical fantasy, means giving away the best of what she has been brought up to cherish and protect. 'If someone would spread out gold and silver in front of me I would laugh like a child. When they put it away I burst into tears. I had gone mad,' says Akbari without raising her eyes from the kashida, her patch of embroidered flowers.

Her voice has no tone, her eyes no sheen, her hair, a silvery mass, has not been unravelled the way it is with women who pamper it and value it. Akbari gave up that luxury more than fifty years ago. When I ask her age she looks up and ruminates: 'May be seventy or eighty.' Time, like her gold and silver has lost its value. What has not is her needle and thread, the skill that she learnt to use as she was turning into a young woman. In every house chikan worked marvels with women weaving their dreams, seeking solace in an activity that slowly turned into a craft and then a vocation.

In the enclosed courtyards of Lucknow homes, in dim rooms

with few windows the girls sat in circles and learnt to make stitches, make lifelike leaves and buds and flowers on cloth. Through the needle and thread they were learning to fabricate their fantasies which promised brighter homes. Little did they realize that a craft so naturally learnt would in time become the mainstay of their lives. 'No one taught us the stitch,' says Akbari whose name tempted people to call her Badshah in memory of the great king Akbar. 'We watched each other and learnt. When I saw bootas on a dupatta I came home and worked bootas on my own with my needle and thread.'

Today after fifty years of stitching she confidently creates leaves and flowers in thread, makes strings of them to look like creepers, spreads them out into a field in bloom. In this pastel world of white and grey and pearl pink Akbari's bespectacled eyes have found a focus as have her hands and mind that has found a quiet balance with work. Akbari is Amma to the 500 women chikan workers who function as a family under the umbrella of an organization called SEWA, the Self-Employed Women's Association. They have found a way to live and to work, and have gained a recognition for their craft and themselves. SEWA has opened a window in lives that knew none.

'*Chaar paisey miley, kharch bhi nikal gaya, dil behal gaya, ghum bhi mit gaya,*' says Akbari. Through SEWA she has learnt to earn her living and to spend it. She has learnt, too, not to forget her pain but to share it with other women who work and live around her. They are all creatures of a similar destiny, destitute or abandoned.

A number of them look older than their age. It is hardship not time that has taken its toll. Munni Jehan is a toothless woman who is fifty and a widow. Her daughter fell in a well, her son died, of tuberculosis. Khurshed, forty-two and greying, lost her husband in the drought of a summer when the entire village starved to death. She came to the city with six children and found a room in a ruined haveli which is now her home. She sits in its dank interiors crinkling dupattas with nimble fingers. SEWA has given her, as many others, a place to be together, to work, be paid for it and be proud of it. It has helped stir in them qualities of leadership, of decision-making, of taking up and fulfilling new responsibilities.

Akbari has realized her own place among them, as Amma, a role more enlarged than is implied conventionally. She is a woman who is not only loved but admired and respected. Says she: 'When there is love, even if it is not of one's own there is no madness. Life with love moves on an even keel.'

Daughter of the Chenars

'Woman is your garb, and you hers'

She owes her gift to them, her ancestors, men of the Himalayan snows, who came riding their horses from Kandahar. They pitched their tents by the river Jhelum under the shade of the massive maples of Kashmir. They were men of God, claiming descent from the Holy Prophet. In her mind, her great-grandfather stands tall, in robes of embroidered silk and a formal turban. He presided over a small empire of his own—fourteen mohallas, fourteen wives and countless dependents. He gave generously of the gifts bestowed on him. And when the time came he gave it all up and went away to Karbala in Iraq. There he lived sweeping the shrine, giving water to the pilgrims. When he died they buried him at the foot of the Imam's grave.

Her father was a man of the world, a vazir of a district, who owned lands, shops, orchards, who lived in a large house with a joint family, rode a palanquin, wore breeches. The heirloom of his ancestors was safe in his wife's hands, a deeply religious woman. The moment she sighted the moon of Ramzan she handed over the keys of her household to her mother-in-law and settled down on her prayer rug for thirty days. She would fast for the month and break her fast with a piece of bread and kahwa, Kashmir's green tea. As did all people in the valley who for centuries had been nurtured by the faith of Sufis and rishis.

When Shah Hamdan, the Sufi, first came to Kashmir, it was just a lake, goes the tale. It was an earthquake that created the river Jhelum. To his khanqah, his sanctuary, came people of all faiths and learnt the way to God through his example. He taught them how to make carpets and weave Pashmina wool caps. When they understood the nature of wool they came to understand the nature of truth and of God. A Sufi was a holy man who wore woollen garments ('suf' means wool); the name also drew from the word 'suffa', a long bench in Medina on which the associates of the Prophet sat, devoting themselves to a life of piety and poverty.

Many of them conformed to the spirit of the Greek word *sophos* and were wise and lived alone. To Kashmir, through the centuries, such men flocked, living in caves in the mountains, wandering by its many streams, mingling with the native people, learning from them, and giving to them. From the Saivaite yogis of Kashmir they learnt the techniques of meditation. Some took to the dress of yogis and vegetarian food.

Nurud-Din, the great Sufi who adopted the rishi tradition, abstained from fresh vegetables and would not even walk on green grass. When once he went to attend a feast dressed in rags and was barred from entering, he returned home and came back richly dressed. At the feast he let his sleeves dip into the dishes. When questioned he replied : 'The feast was not really for Nurud-Din but for the long sleeves.' He was critical of mullahs and their teachings. 'They wear big turbans and long garments,' he said. 'They carry sticks in their hands, they go from place to place and sell their prayers and fasts in return for food.' The message of Nurud-Din was carried on by his disciples; notable among them was Zainud-din whose shrine in Aish-Muqam draws hundreds of devotees even to this day.

'Qabr-parasti,' the worship of graves, remains a sanctified part of the Kashmiri tradition.

Carrying on that tradition Begum Agha stands bowed at a grave in Char Chenar, her favourite spot in Srinagar, high on a hill shaded by chenars, overlooking the shimmering Dal lake and the snow-tipped Himalayas. Char Chenar is dear to her. For here lies the grave of her husband whose memory she continues to revere despite the long years of anguish he caused her. She offers her fateha, the opening verse of the Koran, at his grave before settling down on the rocks for a picnic of chicken sandwiches and green tea spiked, the Kashmiri way, with almonds.

'The soil of this land has been nurtured by the Sufis,' she says, her grey eyes misty. 'The present day Islam is not Islam. It only existed thirty-five years after the death of the Prophet. Our imams were poisoned and killed. Those who followed ran after money and luxury. Our mullahs today continue to be backward. Real religion cannot take root if it is not translated and interpreted. In Kashmir it took an Akbar to revive the old spirit of religion reminiscent of Sufis. An inscription written by his courtier Abul Fazl to be inscribed upon a temple read thus :

> If it be a mosque, people murmur the holy prayer and if
> it be a Christian church, people ring the bell from love
> to thee.
> Sometimes I frequent the Christian cloister and sometimes
> the mosque,
> But it is Thou whom I search from temple to temple . . .
> Heresy to the heretic and religion to the orthodox,
> But the dust of the rose petal
> Belongs to the heart of the perfume seller.

Against such a background, the Sufis of Kashmir lived, meditated and taught. Begum Agha is a child of this environment, that for years has been ventilated by the spirit of bhakti. A woman's life though remained outside its pale. The turn of the century was still a time when Muslim girls were groomed behind veils. 'At the age of seven I was told that I was to be in purdah,' she recapitulates, patting her silvery hair as it blows in the autumn wind. 'I was not allowed to go out of our house, not even in the compound if there was a male servant around.'

Only the maulvi who came to teach her the Koran saw her. A maktab, a religious school, had been started in the house to teach the girls. She was not allowed to go even to the fourth storey hall as all its windows opened out on the road. It was a beautiful hall with a painted papier-maché ceiling, a floor covered with a vast silk carpet, three tall mirrors on one end of the hall and on the other, glass door almirahs where her mother stored her pashmina shawls, her jamavars, her shahtoosh and her fine porcelain. The young Begum loved going up there but would only be allowed in during festivals and celebrations. Her mother would be seated at the end of the room, her long white neck covered with a necklace of emeralds and pearls, her arms full of gold bangles, her fingers studded with rings and her forehead seeming small, hidden as it was, by jewelled tikkas. 'She was such a grand personage,' recalls Begum Agha. 'I would watch her wiping away the dust from the cups and plates with a soft cloth, whispering all the time. Only her lips would be moving without a sound. When I asked her what she was mumbling she told me "my prayers". She prayed all the time.

'She taught me to pray, to recite the suras. In the evenings she would tell stories that I remember to this day. "A woman will be punished if she shows herself before any man. Even if a hair is revealed, that hair would bear a snake in hell" she would say. I used to go around hiding each hair under my veil. When I completed the Koran, it was a great moment for my mother. She held a feast in celebration and gave gifts to the maulvi.'

When her mother died, Begum Agha was only ten years old. There were no other women in the house except the servants. The young Begum was put in the charge of Mrs Wakefield, an Irish governess, who taught her English and needlework; how to lay the table, how to eat, sleep and walk. 'But my mother had already taught me the fine art of eating with my hands and sitting on the ground covered by a carpet,' she says.' Though I could handle a knife and fork and play badminton in our purdah garden, I remained, like my mother, deeply religious. I always went out in a covered palanquin and did what was told to me. When my father chose to marry me to a cousin I acceded. I never let him know the anguish I suffered even on the first day of marriage.'

Her husband was a pampered young man who had come under the spell of the English missionaries. He had picked up their ways and had lost his traditional manners for he had been orphaned as a child. In her notebook Begum Agha painfully recorded the first night of her marriage. 'On the first night I was ill and not fit to share his bed. He did not talk to me or ask me to say a word. He came like an animal, satisfied his lust and went to his bed to sleep until morning. That was the beginning and end of my dreams of a married life. All my life I have been alone.'

Begum Agha went out to teach women. Taught by a private

teacher, she had to begin as a third mistress of a primary school. When she retired, she was the inspectress of schools in the valley. 'Man through centuries has remained hakim, the dominant one and woman mehkoom, subservient. But that is because of woman's own ignorance,' she ruminates. 'How many women know what the Koran says about a man-woman relationship? "*Aurat tumhara libaas hai, tum uska*"—Woman is your garb, and you hers, says the Koran. There is equality ingrained in Islam. Manliness is not to discard a woman but to give her a helping hand. Divorce is displeasing to Allah. Our problem is we don't read the Koran in our own language. Our children today can't even recite the kalma, the Word of God. Woman is not organized enough to stop man's exploitation.'

It took her long years to understand it herself. When her husband married a haanji woman, one of the boat people, she remained quiet. She had dreamt once of dropping a ruby earring in the lake and a haanji woman had picked it up. So when it really happened, she invited her husband to bring her home. 'Are you a Jesus Christ?' he teased. But when he took ill he came to her. She nursed him for twenty years. Her anguish, that she dares not voice, rings in the lines penned by a grandson years later . . . .

> *While her husband*
> *thumbed through Plato,*
> *spending the dialogues like a pension*
> *in whispers, his inheritance*
> *lost, his house taken away,*
> *my grandmother worked*
> *hard, harder*
> *than a man to earn*
> *her salary, from the*
> *government and*
> *deserve her heirloom*
> *of prayer from God.*

Wajida

'To write is like love. The more you spend of it, the more you stir new sources, new energies. To hold back withers, inhibits and ultimately kills the seeds.'

The words are spoken by Wajida Tabassum, a writer of Urdu romances. A warm friendly woman, she sits sprawled on a velvet sofa in a drawing room that looks like a Hindi film set. The comparison is not an idle one; Wajida reveals that she often rents her home near Bombay's Juhu beach, for film shootings. She even writes film scripts and lyrics. She recites a couplet from her latest song:

Ab ke sawan mein hum tum sajanya saath nahanyenge
Bheege bheege kapdon mein tujhe phir khoobh satanyenge
(In the next rains, my beloved, we will bathe together,
in clothes dripping wet we will tease each other.)

Writing songs like these, she giggles, does not qualify her to talk about Islam. She wears no purdah and talks with pride of her MA degree, her travels in the UK, Canada and America, and her efforts to unveil what is suppressed in Muslim society. Her books, she proclaims with a touch of glee, are banned in polite circles. They are not displayed in the showcases of respectable bookshops. She has even heard that those who read them are advised to take a bath to cleanse themselves.

But, she tells people, 'When I write what seems vulgar, the angel above my left shoulder notes my evil act. But the one who presides over my right shoulder also notes my good deeds. Since the age of eight, I have not missed a single namaz. Praying to God is like love. The longer I pray, the better do I know Him.'

In fact, Wajida prays six times a day. 'What takes a normal person five minutes for one namaz, takes me half an hour. My husband teases me that God must panic seeing me unfurl the prayer rug. As my thoughts stray, I repeat each line to squeeze out its best meaning. I have chosen to inflict this punishment on myself as a thanksgiving. So many good things I have learnt from Islam—it has given me shaour, spirit and strength, taught me to forget and forgive, to care for the poor.'

Imaan, she believes, is the best gift God can give to a Muslim woman; she feels fortunate to have been granted it. Once, a bearded mullah told her that no decent person could read her books. She turned back and asked him: 'Why do you with your big beard read them?' She tried to shock him when she said that she herself did not read her books for she considered herself shareef.

'If what I portray is vulgar and filthy, then it is part of life that I observe,' she claims. 'A writer is bound to write what she sees. My stories stem from the injustice that I see around me, the hypocrisies that persist despite the talk of religion. I have seen more women in purdah commit non-Islamic acts than those who do not wear it. It has the quality of rubber. If it is pressed long and then released, it bounces back and even hurts. Some day I have to show my face to Allah, even if I write what is called vulgar. God says He will forgive our big sins if we don't commit small ones. I try not to. I am a very honest woman.'

And because of her honesty, she decided not to wear purdah. For God is Saheb-e-Jamal, the personification of all beauty—to hide what is given by Him she deems a sin. It is to please Him that Wajida exults in her nondescript face that is generously painted with rouge and lipstick, even at three at night, looks at the mirror, and thanks Him for the looks He has given.

'How will God accept your prayers if your face is always made up and you sit with men, people ask me. I tell them as long as I do my prayers, I can paint my face, switch on the video and even watch a movie. There is no purdah between God and a woman. She is closer to Him because she knows the pain. In the process of creation she bears life out of her own life. It is the duty of every woman thus to be honest and a namazi, to say her prayers. Was it not Napoleon who said that if he is given excellent mothers he will give the nation excellent citizens?'

Wajida considers herself one among them. She prays six times a day, gives generously in charity with the hope that she will get back tenfold from God. She is spotless in character, for no man, she confides, has touched her except her husband. These are the essentials that make a Muslim woman. Her acid pen lashes out against the social injustices that her mind has learnt to dissect. But years of conditioning deter her from probing the complexities of a long-buried female consciousness.

She sees no conflict between the Islam she swears by, and her aggressive modernity. She explains it easily: there is one conviction that we inherit and another which we create through our own experiments with truth. The prayer is the same but the manner in her case has changed. How has Wajida the writer evolved her own belief?

'I have my own equation with Allah,' she beams. 'For hours I repeat my prayers till I feel close to Him.'

So, she is critical of women who wear purdah for she finds it suffocating. But she refuses to step out of her house or travel unless she is escorted by her husband. The refuge he has provided is integral to her serenity. How then does she see me, a woman who wears no purdah, who has no husband and who journeys through life alone?

'I see you as unfortunate,' she says apologetically. 'You have been deprived of a husband and children. I feel afraid when I see you travel alone. I may appreciate it but I don't envy it. A married woman who gets the protection of a husband gets used to it and cannot conceive anything else. She is content in her cage.'

I would call such a woman unfortunate, I tell her. For she has failed to know herself. How can a thinking person be content without raising questions and how can a writer really give if she chooses to hold back?

Bano Begum

'Music is my prayer'

Seated on a stage, dressed in a bright green sari, her head coyly draped Bano Begum sings. She is an older woman with the voice of a young girl. She sings of Radha and Krishna, of Mira, the queen who gave up the joys of a palace for the love of God; she sings of forbidden love, of Mecca and Medina. I am intrigued by the songs and the singer. To hear a Muslim woman sing bhajans and naaths with the same gusto seems unusual. I enquire about her and am told that she hails from the Rajput tradition, that she lives in Jaipur, and that she is a maand singer, one who lends to music the decor and pattern which mehndi maandna signifies for the palm of a woman's hand.

Bano Begum lives in a little-known house in the old Chandpole bazar. Unniyaraon ka Raasta is a narrow lane trapped between the stone walls of another time. It is dark here, for the sun recedes faster from this part of the city. A small board hangs on a door bearing a name in small letters. It is Niazi which, she explains, means one who bends before God. And that is the appendage she has adopted as her last name, one that has come to her from her Pir who has shown her the path. Only women with a profession have their names inscribed on entrance plates. Other women—mothers, daughters and wives, are embarrassed with such an assertion.

Up a dark steep staircase, on the second floor, in a bare room Bano Begum is seated with another woman. Her greeting is a deep salaam, accompanied with apologies for the way the house looks. There is no cooler in the room and it is hot outside, she says as she settles down on the farsh, a durrie with a white chadar spread on the floor.

She introduces the other woman. 'My sister,' she says. 'Yes, she too was a singer. But she gave up singing when she completed her Haj two years ago.'

Bano Begum too had once taken a vow to give up singing. For twenty-eight years she kept her pledge, till she fell sick and a doctor advised her to return to singing on health grounds.

Isn't her music more important to her than vows? 'No, no,' she says hurriedly. 'My religion is as important.'

But isn't singing taboo in Islam, I ask. 'We were Hindu Rajputs before,' she admits. 'We converted to Islam because of certain needs.'

She does not explain what those needs are. Others, in hushed tones, tell me later that among singers' families women enjoyed less freedom. Though they were the bread earners, they were not allowed to participate in ceremonies for the dead.

'In Islam there is more equality for women,' says Bano Begum. 'I was only eleven when I embraced Islam. I remember how I was drilled into doing my namaz five times a day and fasting for thirty days during Ramzan. Islam is a religion of rehem, of compassion,' she asserts, with the fervour of a convert.

Will she sing for me I ask, changing the subject. 'Yes, yes,' she readily agrees. 'But may I first do my namaz?' It is the time of maghrib, the evening prayer. In the distance the azaan rings. Bano Begum settles down on a small rug in the corner of the room, draping herself closely in her discoloured grey sari. The room is bare except for a picture of the Kabah, tilted on a peeling wall. Her prayers over, she returns and sits by her harmonium. 'If you had come tomorrow I would not have been able to sing,' she says. 'Tomorrow is Chaand Raat. Muhurrum will begin. We do not touch our instruments for ten days.'

But the mood of Muhurrum it seems has already entered the room. *Chandni si raat* sounds wistful, more poignant in the haze of the hot stuffy room. It is summer inside and outside, a blanket of desert dust hangs over the city. There is no moon. Except in the voice of Bano Begum. It rings with longing, bringing back to life the broken dreams of countless women, who have for years waited for nights of the moon that would make their love visible. The poetry of the songs evokes a world more of myth than reality.

'That's the way women lived in olden times,' says Bano Begum. 'Their sentiments are best epitomized in the songs of Mirabai, the poet-saint of Rajasthan who lived in the fifteenth century. She is the voice of all those who love and in love find their ultimate truths.' She begins to sing a bhajan of Mira.

Papiha
do not sing his name.
If a love-lorn woman hears you
she will pluck your wings
break off your beak,
touch salt to your wounds.
I am his.
He is mine.
Who are you to sing his name?

And in the next moment she wanders into a ghazal that expresses a longing not for Krishna but for Medina.

'Medina jaoun, phir aaoun aur phir jaoun
Tamam umr isi mein tamam ho jaye...'
—To go to Medina, return and to go again,
let all life be this one journey.

That is her prayer and her song

Kum Kum

'Being an actress does not affect my faith'

'Ma, who am I?'

'You are Choti. My daughter.'

'But what else am I?'

'You are Kum Kum.'

And that's what she has remained—Choti to her mother and Kum Kum to those who watch the Hindi cinema. And what happened to Zebunissa? The old name, given to her when she was born, has lapsed away, as easily as the past. Only distant echoes remain—of a place called Hussainabad in Bihar where she was born; of a grandfather, a zealous Shia, who had built a house for himself in faraway Karbala in Iraq; of stalwart men in the family who claimed direct descent from the Imams; and of a house that rang with the fervour of majlises, the gatherings held in Muhurrum, the month of Imam Husain's martyrdom. It is difficult to link Kum Kum the actress with a landscape of such religiosity.

'You won't recognize this room if you visit me in Muhurrum,' says Kum Kum sitting in the large, nondescript sitting room of her suburban flat in Bombay. 'Muhurrum is celebrated in my home the way it always has been in my family. Nothing has changed. My being an actress does not affect my faith. I have been deeply religious since childhood, like my mother. But I also wanted to play, to sing and to dance. My mother never stopped me. She felt it was against nature to curb the exuberance of a child.'

That exuberance remains an aspect of Kum Kum, now in her fifties, and a mother. Her sinuous figure ripples as she walks across the room, her eyes beam, her voice bubbles as she recapitulates that magic time when she sang and danced. 'I was just a young girl when I was spotted by the great director Guru Dutt. I had dropped out of school, in the seventh grade. We had just moved to Bombay. My father had left us and gone away to Pakistan. My mother, who had always been in purdah, brought us to Bombay, single-handedly looked after all of us. I was her favourite. I was lively, my expressions were good, as was my diction. Guru Dutt wanted to cast me in the role of a young woman who lives in a chawl and awakes after a long night of drink. I had never seen liquor, did not know what nasha means. I was reluctant when I was asked to wear only a blouse over a petticoat. But it was a challenge. When I watched Guru Dutt I forgot my fears. I put on a gown to cover myself and walked up for the shot. I removed the gown when the director said "shoot" I put back the gown when the shot was over. I had conquered the first hurdle. Later when I had to play roles scantily dressed I was not afraid. When my first film was released I was acclaimed as a new star. That's how it began.'

Kum Kum sang and danced across the silver screen for many years—a time when she came alive, realized who she was. To see her 'true' self she would sometimes wear a burqa and walk into a cinema hall. She would buy a ticket for the cheap stalls and sit amidst the public whose reactions she wanted to assess. *'Kya zaalim cheez hai,'* the men would shriek when she danced. She soon realized that it was their way of appreciation. The woman on the screen who titillated the crowds was the actress. Back in the house, she was the daughter who would sweep the floor, wash dishes, and cook like any ordinary woman.

'I never had bloated visions of myself,' she admits light-heartedly. 'Even when I had become a star and acted with big heroes I did not demand a separate chair for myself in the studio. I talked freely with everyone, whether he was the producer or the light man. I was a simple girl who went along with everything. And as I had joined films at a young age I grew into my career. I did small roles and rose to the top. I did whatever role came my way, heroine or vamp, comedy or a dance sequence. To say that films spoil you is wrong. You can be spoilt anywhere if you are weak. It depends on your character. If you begin to live life as if it is a film then you are doomed. I lived a normal life. I had my mother and my faith. I had prayed since I was eight years old. I could not pray in the studios but I always did when I came home. I could not fast while I was acting for I was spouting out love dialogues that were all lies. I would pray to God who is all mercy and compassion to forgive me. I was doing my work. That never interfered with my faith. Islam asks us to question things. Films have given me an understanding of life and people. They have given me name, money and self-respect. I feel I am a better person because of films.'

What would she have been if she had not joined the film industry?

'Nothing,' she says flatly. 'An average Muslim girl grows up inside a house. She is taught to read the Koran, to pray, to fast and to observe purdah. She is told not to go here and there. Then comes the D-day and the proposal comes. She is married and enters the house of her husband. She walks as he commands, goes out to a wedding or a funeral but nowhere else. She never really finds out who she is. I believe a girl should educate herself and stand on her feet. She should see the world. It is something to see and experience. There is good in it and also bad. When she learns to distinguish she can lead a fuller life. Though I was born a daughter my mother treated me like a son. I did all that is expected of a son. I bought this house in my mother's name, something a girl is not allowed to do.'

Kum Kum married and bowed out of films. 'She can still act if she wants,' says her husband whom she has known since childhood. 'It will make no difference in our personal lives as long as she bears her responsibilities, takes care of her home and children. I trust her in whatever she does. Hijab is not a mere wrapping to cover a body. It is a viewpoint and how you feel inside. A woman has the strength to do many things. If she has fidelity, if she can control herself, she can be in any profession. Islam encourages people to think and to act.'

Fatima

'Allah is no longer the 100 watt bulb'

'I would jump on a cloud, ride it and float with it.' While women in the family sat around and gossiped in the inner courtyard, Fatima would lie on the takht and watch the white and grey clouds.

She has travelled a long way on the back of these Deccan clouds. I meet her in an ashram miles away from Hyderabad where she was born in a traditional Muslim family. Nothing about her appearance suggests her Muslim background except her accent, sharp as tamarind, the fruit that spikes the foods of her native city.

'Clouds fascinated me,' she says as she wanders back, remembering a cloistered childhood. 'As did the stars. On a clear night they seemed so near that I dreaded they would lose their balance and fall off.'

That was just one of the many fears she imbibed as a child. The family, large like a tribe, gave her love and shelter but no understanding.

'All the women in the house moved around wearing masks,' she recounts. Her voice is detached as if she is talking about distant shadows. 'They never revealed their true feelings, they said what they were brought up to say. Now when I think of them I feel they never really knew who they were. They lived with so many fears that they dared not question. Women grew up afraid of the dark, of being left alone, of people, of the unknown, of Allah. Fear was often the root of a religion in which we were groomed. We were taught to repeat our prayers, to ask God for things and for forgiveness. Who God was I never really figured out. I was not supposed to. I imagined Him as a ten million watt bulb that I was afraid to look at. My Hindu friends could see their God and pray to Him. I did not. I was a restless child. Despite the roots I grew up not being rooted.'

And so she travelled. Like many young people in search of money, work and a new life she arrived in Bombay. She exulted in the heady freedoms the city offered and discovered herself as an artist. She had no home and little money. But many things in the city were free. She enjoyed riding in the crowded trains and buses, haggling in the bustling markets, eating in the wayside restaurants that served basic meals. She made new friends who knew nothing about her family or her faith. Men were attracted to her sultry looks, women were often threatened.

'I could never give myself to anyone,' she confesses. 'I did perhaps sexually but never totally with body and spirit. I felt best when I painted. But when success was instant I rejected it. I found I was repeating my art. Like a reflex action I was painting as if brushing my teeth. I did not build a career as an artist. I rejected marriage; I wanted to build a small house but I stopped. I have no regrets. I was in search of the real.'

That dawned on her on an ordinary morning as she sat reading a book. A line popped out of the page—a thought of Rajneesh: 'To make your presence felt is violence.' That led her to his ashram in Pune. At first she watched it dispassionately, resisting what it offered. Sanyas was an alien concept, it was not part of her background or conditioning.

'As I was entering the Buddha Hall one day a question I wanted to ask was asked by someone else in the audience. "I love you and understand you. Why should I take sanyas?" To this Bhagwan answered: "You invite me and I arrive to find the door of your heart locked." That opened the door for me. I realized that sanyas meant renouncing one's ego. It meant stopping to say "I am", the two words that separate you from existence. I became aware that to live life one needs another kind of consciousness, a deeper awareness of existence. One has to flow with life. Now I know why I wanted to ride a cloud, become the breeze. My past ceased to have a meaning. And the future was yet to be born. All that matters is the present. Each moment is pregnant.'

Fatima took sanyas, garbed herself in robes of saffron, the colour of renunciation and wore a string of brown beads with a picture of Bhagwan Rajneesh enshrined in her necklace. Giving up smoking and drinking, she took to rigorous meditation, an exercise totally alien to Islam. 'Turn your work into meditation, says Bhagwan. When you are in it with your totality your mind drops and you become totally aware.'

To hear her referring to a godman as Bhagwan seems strange. For a Muslim there is no other God but one. 'My whole chemistry changed,' says Fatima. 'I am no longer trapped by any religion. I am aware of the existence around me and myself in it. I love every bit of life. The narrow confines of religion have broadened.'

Bhagwan's book, *People of the Path,* has illumined Islam for her, a faith in which she was born. For the first time, she felt she could understand Islam. Bhagwan saw the various saviours and avatars as individuals, who had flowered and become doors into the unknown. In his words: 'They all have the same taste, the taste of the ocean...salty.' Muhammed was the youngest of these messiahs.

For Fatima Allah is no longer the big bulb but a noor, the glow that the light sheds on everything.

Beginnings in a Graveyard

'Can one worry about the dead when the living are dying?'

There is a graveyard in the middle of the city of Hyderabad — small, deserted, overgrown with weeds. The gravestones bear names that have weathered in the sun and rain. In their time they were luminaries, the Bilgramis.

Among them is my father. His grave, like the others, is unswept, unattended. Over its marble surface, rags dry in the sun. The filigreed marble wall raised by a fine mason is broken. The Urdu couplet that he had written in the manner of an epitaph has faded. The graveyard that was a scene of communal carnage, is filled with silence, not of the dead but the living.

A flutter breaks it. It is a red kite over my head slowly urging itself heavenward. I follow the invisible track of the thread that goes up and then down to the earth. Two young children, brother and sister, their eyes wide, stand under a spacious banyan tree holding on to a fantasy of red paper.

'Where is the caretaker?' I ask.

'She is our mother,' they say. 'And that's our house.'

I see a short green door in one corner of the graveyard. The boy brings down the kite and leads the way, hopping over graves, his feet brushing the weeds, gathering the dust.

'My father is buried here,' I tell them, stopping to read aloud from the tombstone. 'No one sweeps his grave,' I mourn almost to myself. They listen attentively, saying nothing.

'Where is the time to worry about the dead when the living are dying?' says a large woman emerging from behind the green door. Her face is creased with wrinkles, not the kind age inflicts but those that are an expression of her own lack of concern for herself. She does not invite me into her house nor offer a glass of water, courtesies that come naturally even to the poor. She looms outside her door and in a monotone talks about herself and the bad luck that hounds her.

'They broke into my house and took away everything,' she complains. 'Six steel plates, two steel cooking vessels, a quilt, a plastic bucket, everything. We tried to save our lives and took shelter in a neighbour's house. We sat on Reddy Saheb's roof all night and watched them as they trampled over the graves, brandishing swords, shrieking slogans in the name of some Bajrangbali. You must have seen the trash they left behind.'

'Why don't you clean it?'

'When I go out to sweep, the children of the sweepers throw stones at me,' she cries.

She is referring to her neighbours who live across the wall. Living together for years, sharing a neighbourhood, has not changed her attitude towards them. She refers to them contemptuously as bhangis, sees herself as superior, a member of a community, the Shias, who take pride in a culture and refinement, nothing of which, not even a trace, clings to her.

'You live here?' I ask pointing to the green door.

'For twenty years,' she sighs, pushing the wobbly door open. It opens into a bleak cubicle, unfurnished, except for a tattered mat, a few discoloured pots and pans and on the peeling wall a plaque of panjetan — the five names of the Holy Prophet and his family. It commands the same kind of reverence that icons do in Hindu homes. She hurriedly touches the plaque, dusts it with her hand and declares in solemn tones; 'By the good names of panjetan I swear that my house was looted. I had to borrow money to put back a new door.'

'I believe you. You don't have to swear,' I tell her.

She heaves a sigh of relief and stretches out her hand. 'I need money for rice.'

To beg and borrow has become a way of life with her. She is not embarrassed, as if hardened by her life with the dead. She blames it all on fate and on an alcoholic husband. When he returns home after plying a rickshaw all day in the city, the graveyard resounds with her cries and his beatings. He gives her no money, she mourns. She feeds her eight children with the small salary she draws from the graveyard committee and from the charity she extracts from visitors.

Without giving any myself I withdraw. I feel her glazed eyes pursuing me as I move back through the graveyard. I find the young girl under the tree washing her brother's school uniform. He goes to school, she informs me. Their mother won't let her. She wants him also to work in the garage and earn a rupee a day. He prefers school. He walks to it, four kilometres each way. Their mother can spare no money for a rickshaw. And their father sleeps late after drinking and fighting. The girl follows me to the gate. 'I will sweep your father's grave,' she says as we part.

'Aren't you afraid of the stones that your mother dreads?' I ask.

'No,' she smiles. 'Those people are my friends. We play pebbles together.'

Afterword

'Praying in the dark'

 To look for Muslim women I had to travel in another kind of world where the light falls differently. It is a withdrawing light, the kind that one associates with the colour of forgotten streets henched between collapsing walls of old towns; it is the fragmented light that broods in patches in enclosed verandahs and unkempt courtyards; it is the light that filters through curtains, of chintz or cane or tattered sack, and spreads out in shadows, transmuted, transformed. I had thought of this light as an abstraction until I met women living in it, day after day, year after year, entire lengths of their lives.

None of them I soon realized lived on main streets. I did not find even one standing in a front porch or sitting by an open window looking out. I always found them in the interiors. I walked through back doors, crossed courtyards, waited in front of wall-like curtains before I was announced in. Inside lived a world, half light, half shadow. A cloud-like quality pervaded everything—the room furnishings, the faces of people, their manners, old fashioned, weighed down by courtesy, voices toned to a pitch that knew no aggression, eyes lit despite the shadows opening into spaces and feelings, more dream-like than real. Scattered across the land, between geographical and cultural opposites, I met women who shared one state of being, inspired by a religion that was a barometer of their lives, literally from birth to death.

Nayab Jehan, reconciled to the life of a village courtyard, seeking a peace not in this world but in the next did not seem very different in spirit from the Begum of an erstwhile state who had not stepped out of her mansion for thirty years, having found her centre in her own silence. Or the nameless woman in the shrine who had found her freedom praying endless hours, bowed to the ground. As the sun set she stood up, her eyes filled with the blue of the sky, now luminous with the light that had left the earth and lifted heavenward. Like the earth, she too had surrendered. Living in such light I soon reckoned was an act of faith, a state of mind. In it was wrapped the essence of belief, rooted in time, intrinsic to the very nature of Islam.

The word Islam is translated as submission. It is a term that also means 'entering into a covenant with God.' Many of the women in this book have found its meaning without knowing it, by simply living their lives. It is apparent in their nature, not in their brains. Few among them claim to be learned. A number of them have not even read the Holy Koran. All, though, have an understanding of the five basic tenets that form the core of the faith: the belief that there is no God except God and Muhammed is His messenger; that prayer must be performed five times a day at the prescribed hour; that fasting should be observed during the thirty days of Ramzan; that alms should be given regularly and Haj undertaken at least once in a lifetime. Drilled into each of them, these five tenets are as natural a part of their growing up as are the seasons that govern the earth and human life. And over a period, the drill acquires a resonance, reaching the level of instinct.

'Prayer is the best medicine,' says Mehdi Begum. Her home is a hovel four feet square whose only opening, a hole near the roof is covered by a cloth to bar any ray of sun or air. She had no medicine for her dying child, no incense to burn at her funeral. But she had her strength intact to continue praying. 'Dua is bigger than dawa'—prayer has a bigger power to heal than any medicine, she says. But her child died. 'Maybe my prayer did not reach Allah. Maybe I had faltered in my faith.'

More poised in her imaan but equally reconciled to her fate is Begum Nazeer who too lost a son in communal carnage. She was at the lunch table when the news came that her young lawyer son had been stabbed. He was coming out of the mosque after his afternoon prayers. He was on his way to collect papers from the court. He had no reason to be killed. 'It is the will of God. Only He knows why it happened,' says the mother. Is she not angry? With whom, she questions blankly. 'We do not have the strength to know or to understand. He is the best judge. We are brought up to rely on God from the day we are born. It is this aqida, this belief that gives us serenity, the strength to bear.'

Begum Nazeer has read her Koran. She fully understands its dictums. She also is aware of the complexities of the world in which she lives. That knowledge in no way negates the quality of surrender which is inbuilt in her temperament, one that only bows to the designs of God.

'I don't leave him until my prayers begin to make sense,' says the writer Wajida Tabassum. She prays, she claims, six times a day. 'Call it an addiction if you want,' she giggles.

For Sajida Biya in Bhopal, prayer is the only lamp that adorns her abandoned niche. The desolation of her dimly lit house acquires a strange dignity when she stands erect along with her old maid servant to pray. 'Even while I was eating gas I was praying,' she mumbles. 'The neighbourhood was torn by cries of women and children. I sat here with my beads chanting the ninety-nine names of Allah. I was in control. I had the strength to walk out of my door, collect the children in the street and take them to safety.'

Her sister Tayeba Begum would have collapsed after a broken marriage. It was prayer that saved her. She now teaches a group of unlettered women how to pray and find peace. For young women like Sugra who have begun to dream of bigger worlds prayer has become a formal exercise. For impoverished girls like Ameena or the working widow Mahbubunissa the strength to earn their daily bread is more important then praying five times a day.

In Jaipur, Bano Begum acclaimed the keeper of the maand tradition, a school of music that belongs to the desert, prays before she sings. Behind the back lanes of a bazar, in a dark, dilapidated structure she lives preserving an art which has also helped her walk on a path outside her own internal universe.

Will you sing, I ask as we settle down in the haze of her room.

'May I first finish my prayers,' she asks settling down on a mat in one corner of the room. For twenty-eight years she did not sing, fulfilling a vow after completing her pilgrimage. She began losing weight, her hair turned grey, she took ill. 'Do what gives you joy,' advised the doctor. She returned to the Muse, began singing again. As she breaks into *Chandni si Raat* the wrinkles on her face ease. She is no longer the old woman who has not seen the moon. Her voice soars and rollicks beyond the stale air of her room like a multi-coloured kite that I saw the young boy flying in a graveyard. It had its own joy, despite being tenuously linked to the earth by a thread that was invisible but strong. Much in the same way Fatima Ahmed has found her truth having floated out of the enclosed courtyard on the back of the Deccan clouds. Her dreams led her out of her home, her city, herself. She saw new meanings emerge in forms and colours as she painted canvas after canvas. She found money, fame, love, sex, freedom. Bewitched at first and then betrayed she gave it all up and took sanyas in a Rajneesh ashram, rare for a woman born to Islam. 'I gained a new consciousness. My chemistry changed. I was no longer trapped by my religion. Allah ceased being the massive light bulb that I was afraid to look at. He became a noor, the glow that pervades all living things.'

Sanyas for Fatima and song for Bano Begum have helped lighten the journey, given wing to the spirit, which in large numbers of Muslim women remains grounded, still unarticulated. They have no command over it for it is achieved not by knowledge but obedience. In a changing environment such a way of being offers no technique that spurs understanding of realities beyond the individual self. Nor does it help illumine the social order. When you live with a wall around you nothing can enter or go out. When you do not live a truth, it dies. Like praying in the dark . . . .

MORE ABOUT PENGUINS

For further information about books available from Penguins in India write to Penguin Books (India) Ltd, B4/246, Safdarjung Enclave, New Delhi 110 029.

In the UK: For a complete list of books available from Penguins in the United Kingdom write to Dept. EP, Penguin Books Ltd, Harmondsworth, Middlesex UB7 0DA.

In the U.S.A.: For a complete list of books available from Penguins in the United States write to Dept. DG, Penguin Books, 299 Murray Hill Parkway, East Rutherford, New Jersey 07073.

In Canada: For a complete list of books available from Penguins in Canada write to Penguin Books Canada Ltd, 2801 John Street, Markham, Ontario L3R 1B4.

In Australia: For a complete list of books available from Penguins in Australia write to the Marketing Department, Penguin Books Australia Ltd, P.O. Box 257, Ringwood, Victoria 3134.

In New Zealand: For a complete list of books available from Penguins in New Zealand write to the Marketing Department, Penguin Books (N.Z.) Ltd, Private Bag, Takapuna, Auckland 9.

UNVEILING INDIA:
A Woman's Journey
Anees Jung

The women in this book are neither extraor-
dinary nor famous and yet their stories and
testimonies provide a passionate, often
deeply touching, revelation of what it means
to be a woman in India today. They tell of
marriage an widowhood, unfair work prac-
tices, sexual servitude, the problems of
bearing and rearing children in poverty,
religious discrimination and other forms of
exploitation. But they also talk of fulfilling
relationships, the joys of marriage and
children, the exhilaration of breaking free
from the bonds of tradition, ritual and
religion. Taken as a whole, the book is
essential reading for anyone wishing to
understand the women of India—the silent
majority that is now beginning to make itself
heard.

'An extremely valuable investigation into
the lives of ordinary women in India'
—*The Hindustan Times*